How To Put Your Mother In A Home

Professional Skills for a Personal Journey

Amy K. Atcha

How To Put Your Mother In A Home

Professional Skills for a Personal Journey

How to Put Your Mother in A Home,
        Professional Skills for a Personal Journey
By: Amy K. Atcha

Copyright 2013 Customized Caring, Inc.

Cover design by: Wayne Johnson

Published by: Customized Caring Publishing
ISBN – 13: 978-0615930565

For information about special discounts on bulk purchases, please contact Customized Caring, Inc. at 630.306.4480 or www.customizedcaring.com.

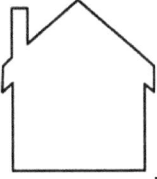

Dedication

This book is dedicated to my mother, Dr. Judith B. Arcy. Thank you, Mom, for giving me the courage, the support and the ideas that made this book possible.   You let me experience the ups and downs, kindness and frustration of life, especially in caring for you. We laughed at times, and cried at times, discovering ourselves – as mother and daughter - in the process of aging. Throughout the days, you were always on my mind and at my side (sometimes literally).

During the past nine years, we have learned a lot about ourselves, each other, and the world. Thank you for sharing your life with me. Thank you for being my mother.

How To Put Your Mother In A Home
Professional Skills for a Personal Journey

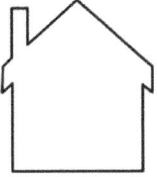

Contents

How To Put Your Mother In A Home

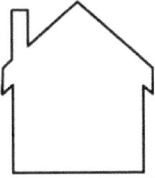

Foreword by Dr. J.B. Hill

As I read Amy Atcha's new book "How to Put Your Mother in a Home" I was drawn once again to the painful memories of the time when we moved Dad to an assisted living facility. Mom had passed a few years earlier shortly after making us promise to take care of "Daddy."

We tried, oh, how we tried to honor her wishes. The problem was that Dad resented our help and we had no clear understanding of the amount of care that he needed. For years mother had been his rock and none of us knew it. My sisters may have sensed it, certainly more than I, but to me Dad appeared to be the decision maker he had always been. In reality, however, he was unable to make good decisions anymore.

Dad lost the ability to handle his check book, operate his electronics, missed Doctor's appointments, got confused while driving after dark, and started having minor traffic accidents. He fell in love with a woman half his age who reminded him of our mother forty years earlier. One day he bought an expensive new bed and with a grin told me that he was "hoping to get lucky." Of course since he was 88, he would have needed more than luck. His comment to me wasn't funny, it was ... disturbing.

After reading Amy's book, I now understand that Dad needed the clear, simplified environment of assisted living. All the signs for this were present. My sisters and I just didn't recognize them. So we did what almost everyone does in this situation. We ignored them and worried about Dad for more than a year.

When we couldn't ignore them anymore, we tried accommodation. We hired a woman to clean house, drive him about, and make meals. Dad fired her. Since it was unsafe for him to drive, we had his license pulled and hired a driver. Dad fired the driver and, to my horror, drove anyway. Finally, Dad became infatuated with a female tending bar at the VFW. It wasn't until he wrote a large check out of home equity to give her for Christmas that we stepped in. Dad moved to assisted living two months later. He loved it.

For the first time in years, Dad was surrounded by other people sharing a common history and enjoying the same things. He dressed for dinner every night --- coat and tie and he rejoiced in the fellowship of happy hour every Friday night. Dad had friends again and he was happy. Mother would have been tickled to have had the opportunity to live there with him. She would have had female friends and it would have relieved her from the burden of worrying about leaving Dad alone.

As a family physician, I have counseled many families about nursing home placement and about assisted living. In spite of this familiarity with elder care, I was unable to separate myself enough to make a good decision about my father. Worse yet, I never considered my parents as a couple and what they might need together. I kept imposing my perception of what I might want for myself on the decision for what was best for them. The indications for assisted living were all there. I did not understand this until I read Amy's book.

I now understand that while I attempted to preserve my parent's independence as I understood it, I was also facilitating their loneliness. Dad, in particular, needlessly suffered from the mistake I made because I did not understand and could not recognize the clear signs that Amy Atcha writes about in her new book. "How to put your Mother in a Home" is a must read for anyone struggling with the decision we all face about how best to care for aging parents.

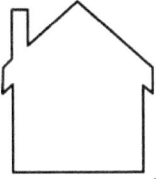

Preface

Last year it was my mom's turn. My mother (aka Mom, Judy, Little Grandma, Grandma Judy, etc.) had been living on her own since her divorce in the 1980's. Her lifestyle and health allowed her to go where she wanted, when she wanted, and do what she wanted. Mom had retired from her job a few years before and was now spending time doing just as she pleased! After all, that's what retirement is all about, right? Dinner out with friends, vacations to see family, trips overseas. It seemed there was nothing Mom couldn't do.

Then life happened. First her vision started to deteriorate, then came the hearing loss. Were these what lead to the car accidents, the irritability, and the vague responses to questions? Only God knows. But no matter what the reason, it was time. It was time for Mom to get the extra help she needed. It was time for Mom to move closer to someone in the family. It was time for Mom to **receive** the support and care that she had so graciously been sharing with us all her life.

In the year 2000, Mom moved to Bartlett, Tennessee, a suburb of Memphis. Her job had taken her there, just as my job had taken me to Chicago, my older brother Dan to Houston and my younger brother Matt to the other side of the world, literally, Perth, Australia. We were at that time, and still are, just like you - the average American family, living in a global world, dominated and controlled by the economy and our jobs.

For the next several years, life continued as usual. We all worked, and had our friends, families and activities to keep us busy. We would talk on the phone occasionally and see each other about once a year around Christmas time. Being Mom's only girl, I kept in touch with her the most on a day to day basis. But even then, in the early 2000's, my calls were only every once in a while, a few times a month. I was busy; she was busy. All was good.

By 2006, Mom had retired. Now she really had her time to herself. Ironically, it was about then that I started calling her more often. Perhaps because I knew I could get a hold of her easier – or so I thought. My calls increased to every few days, and certainly no less than once a week. Most of the time she would answer, we'd chat, and life was good.

Sometimes though, she wouldn't answer – and then I'd start to get concerned. I'd call a few moments later, still no answer. Then again after an hour, still no answer. I seriously began to worry. Where was she? What was she doing? Oh My Gosh, what if something had happened?! I'd begin to get anxious only to receive a call a few hours later asking what I was so alarmed about – after all (as I was told) she was the Mom and didn't need to check in with me before each activity. She had been out shopping and to the movies with friends. Silly me for worrying!

Yet more often than not, I'd worry about her slipping and falling, and no one being there to help her. It's a legitimate concern. After all, ANY ONE of us could fall and need help.

Only shortly after that time, Mom did begin to have some health issues. Her eyesight seemed to be getting worse, and many of the times that I'd call, she'd need to set down the phone in order to turn down the television (which I could tell was blaring loud!) so that we could have a conversation. Over the course of what seemed like only a few months I came to realize Mom was aging. She had some serious health issues and we needed to have some serious discussions. We, my mom, my brothers and I, needed to make some difficult decisions.

I remember hearing stories about the days when relatives all lived in the same little town, marrying their high school sweethearts, raising their kids and sharing Sunday brunch with the whole extended family. Unfortunately, these days are gone. Nowadays, we are lucky to get together once a year, usually over a holiday. We can't afford to stay in our hometown when the company that's putting a roof over our heads and clothes on our backs says it's time to take the management position half way across the country (or the world, in my brother's case).

So what about Mom? What will happen to her? Forgive me for saying, but she is no Spring Chicken; she's not getting any younger. No matter her age in biological years, now Mom needs some help. Help from one of the kids, another family member, or maybe even an outside caregiver. Help with handling the finances, managing a house, and sometimes simply tending to the daily care of herself. That's life. Life is coming full circle.

We start out as babies needing all kinds of love and care and support from our parents. As we age and grow, we learn to be independent, to take care of our own needs and desires. Next thing we know, we're adults – ambling through life on our own.

Almost before we can blink, we're raising kids of our own. We're controlling the day to day tasks, the week to week chores, the all-encompassing responsibilities within our families. We're the ones making the decisions. And we're learning that the consequences and outcomes of these choices are ours to live with – both good and bad. We have jobs, raise families, maintain homes and care for ourselves, physically, emotionally, and spiritually.

Suddenly (at least it seems so anyway), life changes again. Now we're going back in the other direction. We need help with the cleaning. We need help carrying in the groceries. We prefer not to drive long distances or at night. We forget things. We struggle to do the activities we took for granted only a few short years ago.

Finally, whether we like it or not, whether we initially accept it or not, we need the care and support of our children (and most likely others too) to get by with the daily chores of life.

In 2012, my family and I went through the ordeal of moving Mom from her own house in Tennessee to a senior living community in the suburbs of Chicago. We did this not to restrict or confine her, and not to control her life. We did it, with her involvement, because we **do** love her, we **do** care about her, and we **do** want to support her. We lived through some tough and emotional moments, had a few heated arguments, and hugged each other, and Mom, each step of the way.

Now it's my turn to share these experiences with you – so that you don't have to go through this alone. You now have somewhere to look for advice and someone to walk with you through the process.

This book is not meant to distress or depress you. It's meant to guide and support you. It's meant to HELP you, your mom and your family, get through this period of life. It is written to assist you with the task of disassembling and then restoring your mom's home and her life. Rebuilding her life into a joyful, complete and deserved one, that will last her to her final days – and doing it with peace, love, and security.

I should also mention I come with a unique set of skills and an interesting background which may be considered an asset in this type of endeavor:

I am an accountant who, for 22 years, worked as a federal investigator. I spent a substantial part of my career gathering information, asking questions, analyzing processes, systems, companies and people. I compared and contrasted my results against regulatory requirements, cost benefit ratios and personality preferences. Just prior to my retirement from the government, I found my true passion. I became a National Certified Guardian, helping aging and disabled adults maneuver through legal and financial issues.

Mostly though, I am like you. I have a mom and I love her to pieces.

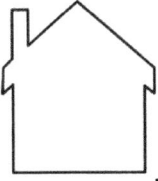

Introduction

The journey of a thousand miles, begins with a single step.
~ Lao-tzu, Chinese philosopher

Moving an aging mother, especially one whose health is slowly deteriorating, is not a one day, one stop event. It is more than simply buying her a new place to live and putting her things in it. Helping Mom move into a "home" is a journey – a journey through the various dimensions of life: physical, emotional, social, intellectual and spiritual. A journey upon which you are about to embark.

This book will give you a glimpse of the journey that awaits you. Throughout the upcoming pages, I'll walk you along, step by step, from the beginning of the path to the end. I will show you the adventure that is involved; the twists, the turns, the various directions from which you, and your mom, will need to choose. I will accompany you, sharing a story, providing information and listing the necessary steps to take, serving as your travel guide through this part of life. On this walk, on this journey, you and your mom will not need to travel alone.

CAUTION! Just as there is no one straight road that extends from start to finish, there certainly is no ONE path for each one of us to follow. Go Slowly! Be aware! This journey, this adventure with your mom, will be full of ups and downs, some pauses and yield signs, some outride bumpy parts, and some smooth sailing times too. While no two journeys are exactly alike, you can learn from the steps that I will take you through.

These steps will make for an easier transition, a smoother passage along the way.

Keep in mind that the reason this trip is even necessary is most likely because your mom's health – either mentally or physically or both – is ailing. With that at the forefront of your mind, you will need to proceed in a way which you may never have done before. THIS journey must have compassion, hope, and trust. THIS journey will require you to remind yourself, and your mom, about why the move is necessary, and that your love and concern for her is the primary objective.

Now, are you ready to push off from the shore? Embark on the journey *with, and for,* your mom. Travel with her as she progresses through the various stages of preparation, ambling along the path of relocating, pausing with questions, and finally arriving at the destination - settling Mom in to her new home.

Pause for one last moment before you take that first step. Ask yourself, again – why am I doing this? Your own motivation in helping Mom on this journey must be one of love, care and concern. Mom will be able to sense, if she doesn't already know, that these are the real reasons you are helping her. If these are not your primary motives, you may want to consider handing the reigns over to someone else. This journey needs someone who will accompany your mom from start to finish, through the good times and bad, with compassion, with patience, and with love.

Number of older Americans

As you get started, rest assured that you are not alone on this quest, nor are you the first to make it.

According to the 2012 U.S. Census Bureau's Profile of Aging America, between 1980 and 2010, the centenarian population (those over 100 years old) experienced a larger percentage increase than did the total population. There were 53,364 people aged 100 or more in 2010, a 66% increase from the 1980 level of 32,194 people.

From the year 2000 to 2011, the population age 65 and over increased from 35 million to 41.4 million. Approximately one in every eight adults in the United States is considered an "older American", with older women outnumbering men (23.4 million to 17.9 million).

Furthermore, a 2012 report from the National Center for Health Statistics predicts that people reaching the age of 65 now have an average life expectancy of an <u>additional</u> 19.1 years (20.3 years for females and 17.7 years for males). Similarly, life expectancy data compiled by the Social Security Administration (SSA) predicts men to be living to age 84 and women to be living until age 86. The SSA report states that nearly one out of every four adults that is 65 years of age today will live past the age of 90, and one out of 10 will live past the age of 95 years.

In 2011, a National Vital Statistics report cited that the overall average life expectancy from birth remained as it was in 2010, at 78.7 years of age.

No matter which way you look at the data – counting from birth or beginning at age 65 – each of us can expect, and should plan, to live to at least the age of 80 years old. How many more years do you have?

Where these older Americans live

If we are going to be alive until we are in our 80's, where are we going to live? And who are we going to live with?

According to a 2012 report issued by the National Center for Health Statistics, almost half of older women (46%) age 75+ live alone.

On the other hand, data from 2011 shows that a relatively small number, comparatively, (1.5 million or 3.6%) of the 65+ population lived in institutional settings such as nursing homes. Note that the percentage living in an institutional setting increases relative to age:

Age	Percentage in Institutional Setting
65-74	1%
75-84	3%
85+	11%

According to the National Center for Assisted Living, there are more than 28,000 assisted living residences in the United States, housing more than 1 million people. The average age of all occupants is 83 years old, and the ratio of male to female is 26% / 74%. The "typical" assisted living resident is an 83-year-old woman.

The facilities themselves range in size from three to 200 units, and provide services for one to 175 adults. The average complex has 43 units; the average number of residents in a facility is 40.

Geographic Distribution

Contrary to popular belief, not all older Americans live in the South, and they certainly do not all live in Florida and Arizona.

The proportion of older persons varies by state. According to the report, "A Profile of Older Americans: 2012" issued by the Administration on Aging, in 2011, over half (51%) of people ages 65+ lived in 9 states:

State	Number of People age 65+
California	4.4 million
Florida	3.4 million
New York	2.7 million
Texas	2.7 million
Pennsylvania	2.0 million
Ohio	~1 million
Illinois	~1 million
Michigan	~1 million
North Carolina	~1 million

As a percentage of population, the study shows that older Americans constituted 15% or more of the total population in the following 11 states:

State	Percentage of Total Population, age 65+
Florida	17.6%
Maine	16.3%
West Virginia	16.2%
Pennsylvania	15.6%
Montana	15.2%
Arkansas	15.0%
Delaware	15.0%
Hawaii	15.0%
Iowa	15.0%
Rhode Island	15.0%
Vermont	15.0%

In addition, 81% of older Americans live in metropolitan areas; with almost 66% of these older persons living outside the city and the remaining 34% living inside the city itself. Only 19% of older Americans live outside of a metropolitan area.

The Trend

According to the National Council on Aging, approximately 92% of older adults have at least one chronic disease, and 77% have at least two. Why is this important to know? As explained in the 2013 report on the State of Aging and Health in America, chronic diseases can affect a person's ability to accomplish important and essential activities, both inside and outside their own home.

As the report further indicates, it might be possible for individuals with a chronic illness to perform, if provided with support services or coping devices and strategies which make the task easier by accommodating their deficit.   Eventually, however, as the individual's health continues to decline, the person may have difficulty performing tasks necessary to live independently. These Instrumental Activities of Daily Living or IADLs include managing money, grocery shopping, using the telephone, housekeeping, preparing meals, and taking medications as prescribed. If the individual's functional abilities continue to decline, whether mentally, physically or both, the individual may even lose the ability to perform the more basic tasks of everyday life. These Activities of Daily Living or ADLs consist of dressing, bathing, eating, transferring (such as from bed to chair, etc.) and toileting.

As you can imagine, the inability to conduct these previously routine and ordinary responsibilities can now severely impede what we would consider a normal quality of life. Without the ability to move, and care for oneself, a person can be significantly limited in terms of social interactions and activities. This directly affects independence and can lead to isolation, unless care is provided in a supervised setting.

As a result of these chronic illnesses, the 2013 State of Aging and Health in America Report further predict that the need for caregiving for older adults will increase sharply during the next several decades.

Caregiving

Now that we know some of the statistics about Mom and her peers, let's talk more specifically about you – the child, and most likely, one of her caregivers.

According to the Family Caregiver Alliance (FCA), an estimated 44 million American families and friends provide unpaid care to another adult. This group of caregivers provides about 80% of the long-term care in the United States. In addition, the FCA suggests that up to half of all caregivers are also working another "real" job, perhaps outside the home. As employees also caring for an aging adult, these individuals can lose work time (and thus wages), and turn down or fail to pursue other career advances and opportunities. Some caregivers, whether willingly or reluctantly, may even need to quit their jobs to provide care to their aging parent.

As you may already know, caregiving can take a personal and professional toll on an individual and his/ her family. Caregivers are at a higher risk for depression, stress, and other health problems. If you're like me, you can probably also attest to the fact that caregivers are less likely to care for themselves and their own health. You'll need to remind yourself at times to take a minute, an hour, or even a day for yourself. Do not think of this as selfish "pampering." It is self-care, and it **is** necessary. Just as they say on the airlines, in the event of an emergency, put your own oxygen mask on first, *then* on the person next to you. You cannot properly care for Mom unless you properly care for yourself.

You may also agree that YOU caring for Mom is a possibility, but not necessarily the best alternative. Mom may need an additional level of care for which you are not equipped or trained to provide. She, and you, deserve better. In fact, you both deserve the Best. And the Best may be in a setting outside your (or her) current residence. This book will provide you with the steps to take when you think a new home may be the best for Mom, as well as how to move her there with the love and support that is needed.

Often times the decision to put Mom in a Home is made only after she has lived with you for a period of time and you (and your resources) have become exhausted. Unquestionably, if Mom does live with you, there will be physical, financial, and emotional strain on you, probably her, and your family. This is a difficult arrangement on so many levels. Yet you still love Mom and you're not sure what to do.

If you are reading this book, then chances are you've come to that point where you feel there is nothing more YOU can do. It's time for someone else to step in to help. There is no shame in this. In fact, you should be applauded for recognizing that you cannot do it all. You should be applauded for reaching out and asking for help. (Why is this one of the hardest things for us to do?)

Do not feel guilty! Either about reading this book or considering placing Mom in a more institutional type setting. You DO care about her, and that is your motive.

How this book will help

If your family is like mine, then you knew right from the start that YOU taking care of Mom in your own home is NOT going to happen. It is not by any means a viable solution. Perhaps it's your travel, your job commitments, your immediate family needs or dynamics. Not all of us are suited to care for Mom as she ages, especially in the way that she needs to be cared for. The reason we can't, and shouldn't, care for her is not because we don't love her, it's because we DO love her. She needs the special attention, and the people with the skills appropriate for her particular ailments. We can give her the love, but perhaps not the direct physical, emotional, social, intellectual and spiritual care that is required.

This book will take you through the process of moving someone you love into a senior living community. This undertaking begins with making you aware of some of the first signs that Mom needs some help, then understanding the different types of communities so you can find the right setting, on to actually making the move, and finally to helping Mom get settled in to her new life. Each chapter walks you through a step in the journey.

Included within each chapter, as the story unfolds, are Steps to Take and Questions for Thought. The steps are designed to make the path on the journey a bit easier to navigate. Each step will bring you and Mom closer to your destination.

After the Steps, there are Questions for Thought - the things you should consider at each cross-road. There are no right or wrong answers. The questions are simply meant for you to think about the different decisions you may need to make or perspectives you may want to consider. Ask these questions of yourself, your Mom, your family, and even your mom's doctors and advisors.

Moving a loved one into a senior living community is not reserved just for Mom. This book and these guidelines are applicable to Dad, brothers, sisters, aunts, uncles, and even a good friend.

The focus of this book, however, is on Mom. Why her? Because she took care of you and now it's your turn to take care of her.

Moms hold a special place in all of our hearts, especially when we are reminded of everything she has done for us over the years. Mom was always there for you, through the good times and the bad, standing as your anchor, your steady post, cautiously guiding you along the way. Now it is your turn to return the favor.

So will this book work for Dad too? Perhaps. However, Moms handle things differently than Dads. With Mom, there is more of an emphasis on the emotional and psychological effects, the feelings – including the aches and pains - and not just the problem solving, analytical side (as is more common to the male point of view).

I, once again, applaud you for using this book as your guide and your roadmap, into the journey of the unknown. Keep this book in a handy spot throughout your trek. Put it at the top of your pack, so that you may refer to it often.

A few words of advice as we begin the journey: Be patient – with your Mom, yourself and the process. You can't accomplish this overnight – it's not wise – either for you or for Mom. A move such as this is a highly emotional journey, especially for Mom. Though with you at her side, supporting her and leading her along, the transition will be a whole lot smoother. You will make this journey not only a professional task required to be completed, but a personal, heart-felt journey, full of support, compassion and love.

It's not going to be easy, but the important things never are.

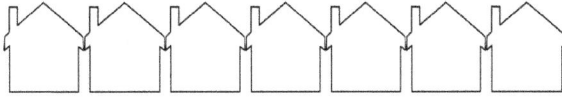

Life is precious. Take care of those you love.

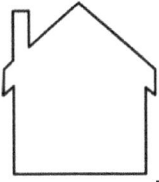

Chapter 1

The Signs

A few more dents in the car.

A bruise or two (or three?) on her arm.

Mom forgot a doctor's appointment... again.

Each one of these is not really a big deal, by itself. But when you begin to see ALL of them occurring, again and again, you can't turn a blind eye.

Sometimes it's hard to see the signs, especially if you are right in the thick of things. Or when you see your mom every day or even every week. Or especially, when you do not WANT to see the signs.

But look again – do you notice any changes in Mom from last year at this time? Is she now standing only two feet in front of the TV, or have it "blaring" loud every time you walk through the door? Is she deferring to your opinion every time you go out to eat? Or getting herself caught up in a discussion, just to avoid actually having to "look" at the menu? Does she keep misplacing her keys? Forgetting to put on her sweater? Or now asking for help to do the things she always used to do on her own?

Getting older cannot be an easy road. My grandma used to say, "Amy, these golden years really aren't so golden". Now that I'm having my own aches and pains, moans and groans, I'd have to agree!

Aging, as I'm now seeing it first hand, is definitely not as easy as it seemed when I was just a kid. At the age of five, you think parents and grandparents are awesome. They have a great life. Mom and Dad have all that freedom - they just go to work, come home to dinner, play with the kids, watch some TV and go bed. No one tells them what to do, what to wear, or that they can't have a second cookie.

Grandparents have it even better. They putter around the house, go on vacations, and of course visit with us – the grandkids. Although their hair is gray and they wear glasses, you don't even seem to notice. They still play cards, sit outside waiting while you run around playing ball, and usually sneak you some extra dessert, all with a silly grin on their faces. That's the way grandparents are, right?

As you grow older, into your teens, you realize Mom and Dad don't actually have it all THAT easy (although at the time, you'd never tell them that). There are bills to pay, kids to look after and a job that makes them tired and cranky when they come home at the end of the day. And it seems like Mom is always insisting (Dad calls it harping) about making those twice a year visits to see Grandma and Grandpa, in addition to the usual holiday trips. You go along; you have no other choice.

When you get to Grandma and Grandpa's house, you think "What's all the fuss?" Grandma and Grandpa look essentially the same. Although, upon further inspection, you do notice that Grandpa is losing a bit more hair, and seems to have missed a few spots shaving. But overall, they seem to be doing fine. You think to yourself, "It must be great to be a grandparent." More puttering, more vacations, and more time visiting with us grandkids.

Not long afterwards, on one particular visit, you sense something is a little off. Grandma and Grandpa are not really doing so well anymore. Grandpa is moving slower and needs more help carrying boxes to the basement. He's acting a little odd too. He walks around like he's looking for something, but can't tell you what it is. Grandma asks you to read her the recipe for tonight's dinner, which of course you do (it's your favorite roasted chicken). You also help her get the cooking pans out of the cabinets – it seems they are too heavy for her to lift now. This all seems pretty natural. You notice it, you help out and yet, it doesn't really alarm you. After all, they are grandparents – their getting old, right? It's just that now Mom gets "emotional" every time she visits with them.

Finally, one day while at you're at work, Mom calls. Immediately you know something is wrong; she never calls you at work. Through her shaky voice and tearful gasps, you hear Mom say, "There has been an accident. Grandma and Grandpa have died." You stand motionless for a minute, thinking to yourself, "What did she just say?"

You come home after your shift knowing what lies ahead. During the next few days, as you watch Mom and Dad struggling through the funeral and the burial arrangements, you begin to see just how precious life is.

Let's fast forward a bit to your mid-40's. Now you're the one putting in the 10 hour days at work, trying to keep up with your kids and their crazy activity schedules, and finally settling in, exhausted, at the end of each day, ready just for dinner and sleep. Time is speeding by too fast. When you do manage to get a minute to catch your breath, you make some time to have dinner with Mom and Dad. As you sit down at the table, you notice – they sure are looking an awful lot like Grandma and Grandpa did when you were only five.

A few days later as you look in the mirror, you detect your own gray hairs coming in much thicker than they did a year ago. It makes you think, "Huh, I guess I'm getting older too." You shrug, that's life.

The next morning, as you're headed out the door, you remind the family that you'll be home a bit later today. It's the first Tuesday of the month, and as usual, you'll be stopping at Mom's house on the way home from work. You and Mom set up this schedule when you moved out on your own, and proudly, you've stuck with it ever since.

You arrive at Mom's door and let yourself in, ringing the doorbell on the way. After your quick hugs and hellos, you wander in to the kitchen. Glancing around, you think, "It sure seems cluttered in here today".

In fact, the house in general seems a bit more crowded than usual. Sure, there is a lot of "stuff" everywhere, but that's how it's always been. Knick knacks from her travels, Christmas presents from the kids. Now though, it looks like things are just not put away or organized the way they used to be. In the kitchen, you even have trouble finding space to pour yourself a cup of coffee. There are pill bottles virtually covering the counter by the toaster, which itself doesn't look like it's been cleaned out in months (or maybe years!).

You don't really notice the toaster, though. Your eyes and mind are stuck, literally, fixated, on ALL those pill bottles! When did Mom start taking all those vitamins? Why does she have SO many prescriptions? Big and small, amber and white vials, most labeled with her name. You think to yourself, "I thought she only mentioned that her blood pressure was high," and "Isn't everyone's when they reach the age of 70?" That's just normal aging, right?

You turn and look at Mom. It's at that moment that you realize just how much she has aged. Cautiously, you ask her about the pills. Reluctantly, she pauses, and then gives you some vague answers that can be summed up to mean that she doesn't really know what any one in particular does. Her doctor told her to take them, she explains. When you gently press her for a bit more information, she quickly adds that she trusts her doctor; she sees him every three months or so. She leaves you standing in the kitchen, coffee cup in hand, feeling kind of numb.

You leave that visit with an uneasy feeling in your stomach, your head and your heart. You wonder, "What will happen next?"

Over the next several weeks, you pay closer attention to Mom and the happenings in her life. You call more often, telling her it's just to say hello. In reality, you're checking to make sure she's okay. Conversations are brief and focus on the ordinary things – what did you do today? What are your plans for the week? How are the kids? Is anything else going on?

After a few months of this, your conversations get a little more pointed. You're sensing something just isn't quite right anymore. You ask how she's feeling, if any of her medications have changed, if she's sleeping okay. Something in your gut is telling you that things are not just "Okay, same as always" anymore. You ask more questions - about her last doctor's visits, her test results, which friend she had dinner with last night and what she ate. You ask what she's been doing to keep herself busy during the day, if she's been to the movies lately or if she's read any good books. When you sense that she is tiring from the interrogation, you pause and let her know you'll see her soon.

Another few weeks go by and it's time for another visit. It's time to really CHECK on Mom and see exactly what is going on. Just thinking about it brings back that nagging feeling – something is not right.

You make arrangements to spend a Saturday afternoon at Mom's house – just you and Mom. This time, there will be no rushing off to the kids' soccer game, no juggling phone calls, no other meetings that have you rushing out the door. This afternoon will be spent with Mom - just talking, and secretly assessing, how she is doing.

You dispense with the pleasantries and catch her up on the kid's school events and activities. You give her the short version of all the drama at work, and let her know that you're doing just fine.

Then, cautiously, you turn the conversation on to her. How is she doing? It's been a couple of years since Dad has passed on (suddenly, due to a heart attack). Mom had some difficulty adjusting to the loss, but over time her mood and her daily routine has improved. Nonetheless, each time you visit, you spend a few minutes reminiscing about him.

At first you are reluctant to even begin this particular conversation. She's been so defensive lately, almost to the point of argumentative. For a quick second you think, "That's just how relationships are between Mom's and kids some times." But it seems like it's happening a lot lately. That isn't right.

You pause and take a deep breath. You tell yourself, "It's time." You need to know how she is really doing – physically, emotionally. No more vague answers; no more general comments.

Turning to Mom you begin asking questions, taking in her responses - both in the words she's using and her attitude and emotion as she answers. You start by asking about the medicines on the kitchen counter. Initially, she resists (again) in this discussion. Patiently you wait, sitting quietly close by, until she begins to talk. She opens up a bit about how she's been feeling, her ups and downs, her health in general, and how she's getting around.

"I'm moving a little slower these days" she says, "but still managing quite fine on my own."

Over the next hour, you cover the bases - from driving, to her recent eye exam, to those nasty looking bruises on her arms. She answers, vaguely, to each inquiry. As she tires of the inquisition, she begins to intersperse the discussion with comments about the neighbors – her attempt to re-direct the conversation away from herself.

You continue to press on, gently, returning the talk back to the matter at hand - Mom. Somewhere along the line, you ask about her finances. Is she keeping up with writing out all her bills?

Mom says, "Yes, you should always be cognizant of where and how you're spending your money". The answer does not surprise you. That is the way you were raised.

But later that afternoon, when you finally get a chance to take a look at her checkbook, you notice it hasn't been balanced for several months. Upon a closer examination, you note that some of the usual entries are not even there.

Without trying to sound accusatory, you ask, "Mom, do you balance your checkbook?"

Her reply, as if you couldn't have guessed it, "Oh, sure. I just haven't in a while".

Your next logical question, "So how do you know how much money you have in your account?"

She responds, rather proudly, that she goes to the ATM occasionally and the balance is right on the receipt. Yup, she's smug; she knows all about technology, ATMs and DVDs.

That's when you look to her desk and see that her computer has a thick layer of dust on it.

"Mom, can I check something on the computer".

"Sure, honey. Go right ahead."

After a quick move of the mouse, and a short delay, the screen lights up, and Mom's e-mail account is displayed. As suspected, the messages have not been opened for over a week, some even longer. You see there is one from the landscaper that she's been using for the past couple of years. Worriedly, you click it open, only to confirm what you suspected - she hasn't paid the landscaper for the last five months.

Very gingerly you ask, "How is that electronic bill service working?"

Turning her attention back to you, Mom admits that it's actually a bit confusing. She can't quite figure out how to print the invoice. In fact, she's been meaning to ask you to help her with that.

You sigh, click on the invoice, hit the print icon and help her out. You say to yourself, "How am I going to handle it when this happens on more than just an occasional basis?"

It's not just the carelessness with the finances that has you concerned. The past several times you've visited with Mom, you've noticed other potential safety issues – her medications are in disarray, she left the oven on for several hours after dinner was done. The TV is blaring to the point that she doesn't hear a knock on the door or the ring of the phone. Since she doesn't seem to use the stairs anymore, there is clutter everywhere, and the bathrooms look (and smell) like they have not been cleaned in many months. Even the kitchen has unrecognizable crumbs on the counter and inside the refrigerator are some items that should have been thrown away many, many weeks before. "Oh dear", you say, shaking your head.

On the drive home that day, you do some serious thinking. You hadn't realized all of these things about Mom. You knew she wasn't going out as much as she used to, even to have dinner with friends. And you knew she spent most of her time just sitting in front of the TV. But when did it get so bad?

Berating yourself, you say out loud, "Why did I not notice these signs before?"

You try to convince yourself Mom wasn't like this a few months ago. Sure, that could be true. But like it or not, it's happening now.

The signs of aging don't hit everyone at the same magical age or even in the same way for each person. For one, it may be the hearing that goes first, for someone else it's the vision, for another it's the memory. The cause of the loss in function may be an acute disease, a stressor or stroke, or simply just biological time itself.

With an illness or an injury, the pain seems sharp and quick. Then in most cases, we heal and go on with life. Except for when we don't …

With gradual aging, the deterioration is slower and can be more painstaking. It happens so slowly that there is almost no way to detect it.

Either way, the result is the same – one day Mom wakes up, and it's time. Mom has aged and she needs some help.

Remember, whether it is "normal age related decline" or something more severe, if Mom needs help, then she needs help. And there is nothing wrong with needing help – no matter what stage of life you are in.

Listed below are a few signs which indicate that Mom may need some assistance. While some of these indicators are strictly physical, others may be compounded markers of cognitive issues or general decline.

> Difficulty walking, or walking too cautiously for the path
> Avoidance or reluctance to use stairs

Bruises on arms and legs
Unusual cuts, scrapes, broken bones

Deferring reading documents (mail, menus, papers, books & magazines)
Difficulty putting the key in the door
Difficulty in using a cell phone or computer (when previously there was no problem)

TV volume is always too loud
Driving issues (dents and scrapes on car, driving too slow, reluctance to drive)

Increase in number and type of medications
Scattered, unmanaged medications – are they being taken? In the correct doses? Is she running out of pills and not refilling them timely?
Change to number and type of doctor's appointments

Generalized change to memory (forgetfulness)
Not remembering appointments
Forgetful / disoriented / confused

Repeating statements (either you need to, or she constantly does)
Speech is less audible, more mumbling or strained
Not responding to e-mails, as she previously did

Not balancing the checkbook
Increase in unpaid bills
Unopened mail piling up

Lack of personal hygiene
Unaddressed urinary incontinence
No longer dressing properly

Lack of cleanliness of surroundings

Hoarding of a particular item(s)

Staying home more; less interactive with friends and family
Significantly less talkative; wants to be left alone
Phone conversations are choppy, vague or cumbersome

Quickly losing temper at failed attempts
Overly sensitive to criticism or disagreements

Significant weight gain or loss (changes in eating patterns)
Changes in daily habits, no longer doing things she previously
     liked

Lack of self-confidence
Depression / Anxiety / Fearfulness over usual activities
Reluctance to do things she used to do

Caution yourself when it comes to the use of cell phones and other technology. These may not be a good indicator of physical and/or mental decline. For many of us in our forties, the constant technological advances can be difficult to keep up with. Don't mistake the reluctance to succumb to all the new features for a true decline in Mom's functionality.

You may stop and ask yourself, "How am I to know what's normal or not?" Or "Mom might just be getting a bit eccentric. Isn't that a part of aging?"

These are very good questions, indeed. If you have concerns of any kind, ask someone – preferably a physician – your own or your Mom's. Professionals can give you the warning signs of aging that might be more particular to your Mom's specific issues and ailments. Do not be afraid to ask. Do your own research too. You, most likely, know your Mom better and see her more often than her doctors do.

If you know what Mom's particular ailment are (i.e. Alzheimer's, kidney issues, etc.), you can also contact related professional associations, either by phone or via the internet. Many of these groups have information for the family and/or caregivers of an afflicted person. They can provide you with the likely symptoms that indicate a decline, and tell you when it is time to seek emergency help. They can also provide you with ways to modify activities or accommodate for any challenges Mom is having.

If you are like me, and think this sounds sneaky and underhanded, think again. You are not interfering with Mom's life or "going behind her back". If your intentions are good, and you are only trying to do what is best for her, she will thank you later.

At some point you will need to discuss your thoughts and concerns with your mom. Just be careful as you address these signs with her. She is most likely going to become defensive. She may view this as you challenging her intellect, her independence, and her pride.

But talking to mom about these signs is just the beginning. Speak with family and friends. Seek out ways to accommodate her deficits. Offer assistance and support.

Remember, though, when you are having these discussions, she is still your Mom. While you do need to be open and honest with her, you also need to be cognizant of how she is feeling. Be respectful. Be patient. Be caring. And tell her you love her.

Steps to Take

1. Write down on paper the specific signs you've noticed that have your concerned. Consider physical, emotional, social, intellectual (cognitive), behavioral, and safety issues.

2. Write down all specific accidents, injuries, etc. that Mom was recently involved in. What role did she play in these? How did she react after the incident?

3. Visit Mom, or have family or friends visit, at least once every few months. Note down concerns after each visit.

4. Discuss your concerns with friends and family to see if there is agreement.

5. Respectfully discuss your concerns with your Mom. Write down her comments and responses.

6. Make a note of any significant changes that have been made (bad or good) over the past year.

Questions for Thought

1. What signs have you noticed?

2. Are these true signs of decline in health or mental functioning that require help? Or just eccentricities?

3. If you don't live near Mom, is there someone who can check in on her?

4. Are you the only one that sees these signs and thinks there is a problem?

5. What things has Mom indicated are causing her concern?

6. Has Mom had any unusual injuries lately?

7. Is Mom missing out on daily activities?

8. How has Mom's behavior changed since last year at this time?

9. Is Mom ready to talk about these signs?

Chapter 2

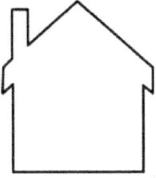

Her Agreement

The signs are all there. Mom definitely needs some help. Now, it's time to figure out who will help, how you're going to break the news to Mom, and how you are going to get her to agree.

From as far back as I can remember, I was taught to be independent. Initially that meant picking out my own clothes and dressing myself. I then graduated to deciding what classes to take in school, then to driving myself into the city, and even what apartment to live in. Next came the decisions of what job to take, who to marry, how many kids to have, and how to raise them. All of these are choices that, while we usually get someone else's opinion (requested or not), we are still responsible for the final outcomes on our own.

Think about it for a minute. Mom has been making her own decisions for 60 or 70 or even 80 years. And NOW you want to tell her she can't drive her car anymore? She can't go to the store by herself?

If you're like me, then the situation went like this…. When you first approached Mom with your concerns about her safety and her "financial issues", she was angry and hurt. She thought she was doing "okay". There was a lot of tension in the air for a few weeks. But you persisted and eventually she did admit that handling the housework, the finances, and herself, was getting to be a bit overwhelming. After a few more talks, and some caring hugs, she agreed that you could help.

Recently, however, things have escalated to the point that you can no longer handle it on your own. For the past several months you've been helping her on weekends and evenings when you can. You were fine doing her grocery shopping and cleaning the house. Now, though, she requires more help than you can give her. She needs help with the daily activities, including bathing, and dressing too. It's time to look for other alternatives.

Let's face it. You knew this time was going to come. You sigh (again). You just didn't think it would be now.

You know it's not a question of whether she needs the help, but rather WHO will help her, and WHERE she will live. Her living in her own home is no longer safe, nor is it convenient for helping her almost every day. But convincing Mom that it is in her best interest to change her living arrangements is NOT going to be easy.

Talking to Mom about moving is going to be difficult, emotionally, no matter when or how you do it. All I can offer are some ideas on what might work better than just the proverbial slap across the face followed by a statement of "You're Getting Old, Mom!"

I can give you hundreds of instances when discussions with Mom about her moving to a "safer" environment is *not* a good idea – Christmas time, her birthday, your birthday, Thanksgiving, essentially any and all holidays, after the death of a family member or close friend... the list goes on. Basically, there is NO good day to sit and have this conversation with Mom. But it must be done.

Don't get ahead of yourself now. Before you go so far as to actually talking to Mom about her impending change, it's best to sit yourself down and think through what alternatives you (and Mom) might have, why these alternatives are worth consideration, and how Mom might react to each of the suggestions you make.

Where do you begin? Let's start with what you know: Mom needs some assistance. The extent of the assistance required depends upon a variety of issues, including what type of support is needed (medical versus non-medical), how often, and what the ramifications are if she fails to get help. An analysis or assessment of her particular issues is the place to start.

Describe for yourself (get your own thoughts straight as best you can), then for your family, your Mom's doctors, and any other caregivers, the following:

What are your specific concerns about Mom continuing to live where she is? Why? Don't forget to include the emotional and social ramifications of her living alone.

Are there safety issues involved, either for Mom and/or for others? Consider the risk of falling or harming herself, burning the house or her clothes, car accidents, forgetting medication or financial issues such as failure to pay her bills.

What alternatives exist at her current house? Is in-home care a possibility? Or is residential care required, either in an institutional setting or a shared or group home?

How much supervision does she need? Is it all day? Can she be left alone while you go to work? What happens if you travel? Who watches over her then?

What types of assistance would be appropriate? Depending on the circumstances, support may include adult day care centers, companion care or nursing aides, and daily money managers to handle the financial piece.

What is the financial impact of each decision? What are the daily (or hourly) costs of someone helping in her home as compared to the monthly cost at a residential facility?

What will be the emotional impact of each choice? What will be the physical impact of each possibility? Consider both the effect on Mom, as well as the effect on the family.

As you are assessing the dynamics of her situation, let's also contemplate the alternatives for Mom. There is a range of care possibilities that spans from essentially no additional work/concern to moving her into a fully supervised environment. Here is a typical path of progression in terms of providing assistance.

Continuing routine safety and caretaking checks by family

Taking Mom to an adult day care

Hiring outside caregivers to come into her current home

Hiring live in caretakers at her current home

Moving Mom into your home (or with another relative)

With or without hiring outside caregivers to assist,

Moving Mom into an appropriate senior living facility.

Ask yourself, what is the best scenario? What is the worst? How will each alternative affect and assist Mom? Positively? Negatively?

Basically, you have five options from which to choose. The first one, however, "Do nothing different", is really not an alternative at all. So let's cross that right off the list.

~~Do nothing different~~
Mom goes to a senior day center
Care comes into the home
Mom moves in with you
Mom moves to a facility

As with any choice, there are advantages and disadvantages. There may not be any one perfect solution, and there certainly is no one size fits all solution. When weighing each option, consider the following:

The additional emotional, physical, financial and time commitments needed to care for Mom.

The structural layout of the environment, i.e. stairs, rugs, lighting, ramps, wide doorways, restriction from stove/ ovens.

The additional emotional and physical stress placed on family members if you're taking care of Mom in your own home.

The cost of hiring outside assistants – either for day sitting or 24 hour support.

The cost of moving Mom to a facility, including your time visiting with her.

Mom's acquiescence or disapproval to the change.

So now you've figured out what YOU think is best.

Don't talk yet! You need to think more ... this time from Mom's point of view. Consider, did Mom ever talk about moving into a retirement community or getting help when she needs it? If so, try to remember what she said about it. Did she like the idea of being somewhere that others could easily help her out? OR was she very adamant that she never wanted to go into "a home". Have her thoughts changed over time? Ideally, the thought of moving into a senior living community will not be a surprise. In fact, many older adults consider moving to retirement communities sometime in or around retirement age. If your mom has already explored this option, then use that to your benefit.

It's been my experience that if a person has made up their mind that they will never go into a nursing home, then they are pretty certain to stick to that decision - at least if they are the one making it. However, if at some point she was open to even considering a move to a senior community, then at least you have a place to start.

Finally, only after you've thought it through yourself, can you introduce the subject to Mom.

I would suggest that you do not just simply wait until she introduces the subject. Chances are, by the time she *feels* that her health has declined enough to need support beyond what she can do alone, and accomplish with your assistance, she is already well past the point. She probably should have gotten outside help long ago, but you thought you could handle it (and you did for quite a sometime). But now it's time for some professional expertise or someone unrelated to step in and take over.

Caring for an aging parent, especially while you are still working and caring for your own family (including raising children) can be a recipe for pure exhaustion. Yet, if you are still uncertain about moving Mom into an institutional setting, then consider bringing Mom in to live with you for a while. Do you think it will ease the burden of knowing she is being looked after? Will it take care of the health and safety issues since others are there to watch over her?

You may also consider having Mom live with you on a temporary basis. For how long will be for you to decide. After the novelty of the arrangement wears off, and real emotions begin to show, re-evaluate the situation. How is the extra person in the household working out? Is it TOO much stress on the family? Is Mom getting the assistance that she needs?

Without question, be careful not to feel as if you are punishing Mom, either by having her move in with you, or having her move into a senior home. She will think she is a burden on you, your family (and even in some cases, society). This will only lead her into being apathetic or depressed. No one wants to be a burden on anyone else.

You might say, well, she already is a burden – and that might very well be the case. So is moving her in with you going to increase that burden? Or make things easier in terms of your time and your stress? Weigh these answers against the financial cost of her living in a residential care setting. Does that change your answer?

My guess is, however, that if she is a burden to you, she likely does not even realize it. You might be able to delay moving her if you can have a frank discussion with her about where the boundaries lie with you helping, outsiders helping, and her having to do more for herself (if that is possible, of course).

Another thought as to how Mom will react to your remarks about her needing help is whether or not any of her friends are in similar situations. Where do her friends live? If she moves into a senior community, will she still have access to her friends in the same or a similar manner to what she does now? Has she spoken with her friends about the possibility or the need to have outside caretakers? You can find out the answers to these questions either by asking Mom directly, or by speaking with her friends – or both! Just remember, if you speak with her friends – she will find out. Do not try to fool her or go behind her back. This will cause more stress and more resentment. It can also delay the move, and possibly getting Mom the care she needs.

Now let's add in a third set of opinions: those of her doctors, current therapists and other specialists. For each of these professionals, it is best that you go to appointments with your Mom to see how she interacts, and so that she may give consent for the release information to you (health information is protected by federal law). If you cannot physically go with her to an appointment, see if the doctor will provide you with a status update either via phone or a written report. It is really important to understand how Mom is doing in the ordinary course of her day, without your biases. An outsider's professional opinion can help to establish whether Mom does need additional care, and what type of care would truly be best for her (not just to ease your mind).

You've gathered some information. Now it's time to talk to your family. What opinions do they have on the situation?

If there is any consideration to having Mom move into your house, an extra step is definitely needed. Before moving Mom into your house, discuss with ALL the occupants of the house (spouse, children, baby-sitters, etc.) what potential changes will be taking place and what is expected of each of them in return. Having anyone move into the house can be cause for disruption. Having your mom move in, AND need additional care and assistance, is a lot to ask of any one person or any family. It will change the dynamics of the living environment.

Consider too, your extended family; your brothers and sisters. It is best to have a family discussion about Mom and what your thoughts and concerns are. If you are united as brothers and sisters with the objective of getting Mom into the best living arrangement possible, then it will also ease your burden. You won't have to feel like you need to do it all, if you have family members that can (and will) support you physically and emotionally.

Last, it will be time for you to have that very candid discussion with Mom. This talk is specifically about her moving. I caution you here: she may not LIKE the changes that are going to take place. While most people will enjoy having someone help them out if they need it, others will not appreciate being TOLD what they will now be doing. Tread lightly. Think about what you will tell her, and how. Think about how she will react to your chosen statements. Patience and soft words will go a long way in easing the transition.

After all of your review, analysis, guidance and advice, you have determined that it is best that Mom move into a senior living community. The reasons for this move you noted for yourself, your family and her professional care team. The reasons for this final decision will vary from one individual to another and one situation to another. Suffice it to say, that in this case, it is the appropriate decision.

With a mixed feeling between relief and dread, YOU have been selected by your family as the spokesperson to break the news to Mom. You must decide when, where and how to tell her. If all goes well, you, your Mom and your family will be reassured with the decision and the discussion. It is the right thing to do.

First up, when to tell Mom. As I mentioned earlier, there is no good time for a discussion like this. Although there may be preferred or more appropriate times to have such a personal and serious talk. The best occasions include when you are doing your own long term care and estate planning; a few weeks after the death of a family friend or relative; after someone you know has had a serious health issue, especially if he/she now needs additional care, etc.

Remember, this is going to be a sensitive and emotional conversation. Try to plan a good time to have the talk. Allow at least an hour, and make sure there is no pressing event to attend to immediately afterward – for either you or Mom. Expect that Mom will show frustration, confusion and perhaps even anger during the conversation. Be prepared for crying, defensiveness, agitation and possibly even a bit of yelling. For yourself, bring some Kleenex (it won't be easy for you either), and your patience.

You may find it easier (or necessary) to present the subject more than once. An initial "overview" discussion to let her know what is on your mind can take place. Then give her some time - a day, a week, even a month. Let the idea of her moving settle in with her for a while. Of course, the amount of time you can give her to absorb the initial "shock" will need to be balanced against her cognitive, physical, and emotional condition, as well as her safety and need for assistance.

Once you have decided when to have the talk, then you must decide where. You know your mom best. Is she a private person? Then have the discussion at home. Does she prefer to get significant news or have serious discussions in a coffee shop or at a restaurant (some people feel they can control their emotions better in this environment)? Find a place that is not too noisy and not too crowded.

Some "less than good" places for you to initiate these discussions are when you're alone with her while driving in the car or standing in line at the grocery check-out. Why, you might ask? The initial response, at least in my experience, has been similar to that of a 5 year old having their favorite toy taken away. It isn't pretty. Emotions are high, and you cannot multi-task.

Consider other dynamics – is it best to have another family member present? Or one of your mom's friends? Do you want to sit together on the couch or across the table from each other? If you are going to talk to Mom with another family member, it is best to have one person across from Mom and another next to her. (If both of you are across from her, she may assume you are "ganging up on her", as opposed to serving her in her best interest.) Even if other family members are not present at the time you meet, let Mom know that the whole family is concerned, and is open to discussion (if that is true, of course).

Last, but certainly not least, you need Mom's input on the matter. Since she is the one at the center of this situation, she should have a voice. Listen to her ideas, her thoughts, her concerns, her preferences. If she is able to share them, then consider what she tells you. If at all possible, do not make decisions without first giving her a chance to discuss the matter. Her agreement to the change will flow much more smoothly if she is involved in the decision, and if she understands why the change is happening.

An ideal scenario would look like this:

Mom has had a few accidents, either in her car or at home. There have been other safety concerns noted too – the stove left on and unattended, Mom tripping over the carpet and misjudging the distance of the curb, medications not being renewed and taken as prescribed, and more than just general forgetfulness (lost keys, forgotten names and recent events), etc. and a lot of irritability. The house is in a constant state of disrepair and clutter. The extra bedrooms are just piled with "stuff", most of which she says she's going to take for donation (but it never seems to get there). The kitchen counters and dishes are not "clean" even though Mom insists they are. Finally, there are several bills on the desk that are stamped "overdue" or "third request". The decision is made that it is best for all concerned that Mom stop driving, that she no longer live alone, and that she move into a senior living community.

After discussing the matter with your family and her doctors, you, along with your brothers and sisters, sit down at the table with Mom over a hot cup of tea. You are direct with her, and tell her, point blank, that you have a serious matter to discuss with her.

Over a cup of tea, begin the discussion by telling her how much you care for her and her well-being. Let her know that you care, and that is why everyone is there with you. Tell her you've been concerned for the last several months about her safety (and the safety of others) because of the accidents, her forgetfulness, and her current health.

Give Mom some time to absorb what you have just said (this is where you stop to sip on your tea for a few minutes).

When the initial shock has faded and the atmosphere has settled, ask her what she thinks? Does she have concerns?

Only after she has had an opportunity to voice her thoughts about what has happened in the past few weeks or months, will you bring up that it is time for her to have some assistance, some help, beyond what you are already providing. Remind her that everyone is going to need help one day, just as we needed help when we were growing up. It's the circle of life, so to speak. Let her know that it's okay, in fact, expected, that she will need help – as you (and your siblings) will one day as well.

Again, pause to drink your tea. Give her more time to absorb what you have just said. She (and you) may or may not need some Kleenex at this point too.

Let Mom know that she will have a say (some input) into the type of housing arrangement she will need to move in to, as well as all the amenities that come with the new environment. Tell her – it is not just YOU making a decision and HER having to live by new rules. Her opinion and consent (or assent) is important too. You will make the decision together.

Plan some dates, a week or so later, to visit a few senior centers. Write down any questions she might want to ask at the facilities. Be open to listening to her and her concerns.

Stay with Mom for the next few minutes (or hours) and find other things to discuss. Finish your tea. Let her know that you always have an ear for her, and that if she has any questions and/or comments, she should be sure to share them.

A hug is great way to end this conversation. Now give her some time.

Let's talk for a minute about consent versus assent. Consent involves her granting permission, her taking part in the decision. Assent differs in that she may only have the ability to express agreement (or displeasure) with the idea, as opposed to taking an active role in the process. Your mom's giving of consent versus assent will depend on her cognitive abilities. If she is suffering from some sort of dementia, she may not have the ability to give consent. Likewise, depending on her level of decline, she may or may not be able to knowingly assent to the change either.

If Mom's condition is such that she does not have the ability to even assent to the changes, then it is likely that a Healthcare Power of Attorney would need to be in effect, or guardianship is required.

Someone, other than Mom, will need to make the decisions. Nonetheless, you should inform Mom of the upcoming changes.

There is no specific rule as to the amount of time you should take to discuss the options which are appropriate for moving Mom. Likewise, there is no specific rule to the number of conversations that need to occur. Regardless of how many times the matter arises; remind her that it is in her best interest – for safety and health – that she move. And of course, remind her that you love her.

If your mom still has most of her facilities, she is likely to have one of two reactions: 1) she completely understands and has already begun the process of seeking help, or 2) she is glad you are stepping in to help her (she was reluctant to ask but wanted the help).

However, if Mom does not quite understand the realities of the matter, she is very likely to be offended and defensive. This reaction, which does involve anger, crying, resentment, yelling, etc. is most likely due to her own refusal to accept her decline – either mentally or physically – and the unsafe consequence that come with it.

If this is the case, think of the 5 stages of grief – denial, anger, bargaining, depression and acceptance. Be patient. She will need to go through all of these emotions. After all, it is a time of grief – grief of losing independence, of realizing one's own mortality.

A few other pieces of advice:

Do NOT just buy Mom a new place to live, and then TELL her she has to move there. Likewise, do not simply move Mom in with you, without first discussing the situation with your family.

To make the situation more appealing, sell Mom on the advantages of the senior living community – both in general, and with respect to the certain type of home that she would likely move in to (i.e.no yard work, no housekeeping, no cooking!). The various services offered at each type of housing are discussed in the next chapters.

Let Mom know that, to the extent possible, you will move as many of her things into her new home as you can. This could include not only clothes, pictures and knick knacks, but also furniture and appliances.

If possible, start early with the conversations – long before it becomes an immediate need. Take your time. Let Mom adjust to the idea, to the plan, to the process. Let her gradually go through all the emotions (and the five stages of grief) BEFORE the day comes to actually move.

Although you hope for the best, you must also plan for the worst. Even as kindly and lovingly as you approach Mom, she may still be in denial and/or offer up some resistance not only to the concept but to the move itself. If this is the case, remember, you are not alone.

Before the air gets heated up and things get out of control, think back to Mom's position. She's lived by herself, sufficiently enough, for the past how many years. She feels threatened, and perhaps depressed, with the knowledge that now she will need some help AND that her current living arrangements are just not suitable for her needs anymore. It will take time for her to accept this. She needs the time to grieve.

So, give her time. If you can, start the process of discussing possible options long before they are acutely needed. If there is time, have the "what if something happens to you?" conversation. Ease her in to the process.

Consider her opinion and her thoughts. Do not dilute or dismiss them. Her feelings are real to her. You are upsetting the apple cart. In her mind, she may know that it is for the best, but her heart is still not ready to let go of her past.

Let her scream it out, yell, fight, etc. You, however, need to remain calm. Do NOT argue back with her. Just keep reminding her that your thoughts are of her safety and her health. You are NOT trying to control her life or punish her. You are NOT trying to upset her. You love her, and you want the best for her and the rest of the family.

You may need to be a little blunt if she insists on you taking care of her. Realistically, you cannot simply quit your job to take care of her. That is the job of a professional caregiver.

If there is conflict, you will, unfortunately, not resolve it overnight. It will likely take several discussions, along with family and friends, before any final decision is made, and before the next phase of the journey can begin.

In getting Mom's agreement to the move, you will be miles ahead. The entire process will be easier and more enjoyable (although still a journey) for both you and Mom. If she has agreed in principal, then she will be more accepting of the change and the remaining steps that come with it. Let her know that she'll be involved throughout the process, and that you will be there by her side.

Steps to Take

1. With your list of signs from the last chapter, talk with your family members about your concerns.

2. Attend (or speak with) Mom's doctors' appointments to see how she engages in public, and to see if the professional care team shares your concerns.

3. Plan, with your family, who will be the spokesperson for discussions with Mom and with her care team.

4. Plan where and when to talk with Mom.

5. Set aside at least one to two hours for the discussion with Mom.

6. Clear time in your calendar for additional discussions.

7. Make time in your calendar to take Mom to look at some senior living communities.

Questions for Thought

1. What are the specific reasons for Mom to move versus getting assistance in her own home?

2. Who will talk to Mom about the decision to get her help?

3. Who will talk to Mom about moving her into an appropriate living community?

4. When is the best time(s) to approach Mom with the subject?

5. How will you handle the situation if Mom is reluctant (or refuses) to agree to move?

6. Do you need to get Mom's consent or just her assent?

Chapter 3

Location, Location, Location

The "Home".

Just what does that mean?

For many, an "old people's home" brings forth images of an old, urine smelling, tile floored, nursing home, with wrinkled, drooling, smelly, unkept patients in wheel chairs, lined up in hall ways, accompanied by crabby nurses and uncaring doctors. At least that's what I remember from when I was 10 years old going to visit my Great Aunt Ruth. The drab institutional corridors with gray painted walls, paper scattered nurse's stations and always, always, always an old mop bucket sitting in the corner. Even the stoic nurses were drab and depressing wearing their slate blue scrubs – no wonder they were cranky. In a nutshell, "the home" is where you went to die.

Today, times are different. The "Home" could mean any sort of place – from the basic, still institutional-looking skilled nursing facility to an elaborate, colorful, resort style senior living community. And let's not forget the cheery assisted living centers and memory care wings. There is no one single type of "Home", just as there is no single type of house for all of us, or even one single type of person that will live in each of these places.

The "Home" you are looking for should truly be a 'home' to your mother, in every sense of the word. It should exude qualities of friendship, companionship, safety, warmth, and hospitality. It should exhibit uniqueness with her own likes, color schemes, pictures and figurines, if you so choose, that is. It should express the personality and beauty of the individual living in it!

With so many options out there these days, just where do you begin? The quest for the right "Home" for my mom began on the internet – as almost all searches do these days. Although Mom claimed she had started "looking" several years before, here and there, while on her travels around the country, I don't think she was necessarily very serious or determined to really find a new home. Things at that time were good for her being just "status quo". However, once her health began to decline and her decision was made to move into a senior community, the search became real. The search became genuine, and so did her feelings toward it. She needed to, and did, treat this pursuit like an adventure, not a chore.

Guiding each other along, Mom and I both started searching for places in the west suburbs of Chicago. We had picked that specific area simply because it is near to where I live. Our goal was to find the perfect place, the perfect "home" within a 30 minute drive of my house.

A quick warning about internet searches: ALL the websites you review will show beautifully manicured lawns and landscaping; the facilities will show blissful, smiling, walking (a few sitting) aging adults dressed in fine clothing, leisurely strolling about and talking casually with each other. The support aides in the pictures all have cheerful smiles, crisply pressed uniforms, freshly painted faces and perfect hair. Don't get fooled. Much like all advertisement, these are the ideal – not the reality. Try to see past the "marketing" and look to what you really need to know – the support services provided and the amenities.

Mom and I considered looking at the places closest to my house, thinking it would make life easier for me to visit. Although there were some of the larger and well-known facilities in the area, many were not the right type of home. As we found out, some complexes are only for assisted living, the type that caters to persons that are impaired to the extent that they need assistance with activities of daily living. Others were specialized units for Alzheimer's patients. Still others were solely independent living communities. None of them were just the right fit for Mom.

You see, my mom is a very active person, and in her mid- 70's, but she does have vision issues. She is still able to manage day to day on most things, provided she has some help with the more complex tasks that require eyesight.

My concern though was deeper than that. Although Mom could manage okay today with limited assistance, what will happen if (or when) in the future she lost all her sight? What if she needed to go from an independent living environment into an assisted living area? And although her cognitive abilities are currently quite strong, what about if (or when) they begin to fail and dementia sets in? Would our search need to begin again – looking for another new home that would accommodate Mom's changing needs?

We decided to take the time on the front end of this adventure and seek out a community that provided a continuum of care – a complex that offered independent living as well as assisted living. That way if (or when) her vision did deteriorate to the point that she needed 24 hour support, it would be an easier transition for her to make - all in the same complex, although possibly in a different apartment or part of the building (and only if appropriate services could not be brought into her first unit).

I remembered years back when my grandmother lived in a Continuing Care Retirement Community (CCRC) near Washington, D.C. It seemed to me to be the perfect concept – staying within the same complex and having the ability to increase the level of care as needed. She had available everything from full independence (with a parking spot!) to full 24-hour supervised care in a skilled nursing unit. This worked well for Grandma since she only wanted to make one more move, rather than, potentially, a series of several.

Keeping Mom's vision issues at the forefront, we narrowed our search. Now we were looking for a place that offered independent living, WITH certain necessary services (and amenities, but we'll discuss those in the next chapter) available such as prepared dining service and transportation, AND with an associated assisted living wing/area for if (and when) Mom would need the additional support as her vision declined. That was our goal. Having the memory care/ Alzheimer's unit and the skilled nursing unit parts would be a great addition, however, that was not a requirement at this juncture (we won't know if Mom will need either of these types of services, but we decided to cross that bridge when we got to it).

Now that our search was more narrow, we selected a few communities from a simple Google search and picked a day to start our on-site, in person tours. We set aside a Saturday to visit three or four places. We had done our leg work on-line and written down our list of places. From what we could determine we had selected the top possible choices that fit mom's needs. We did not make any calls ahead of time to schedule tours or talk to representatives. This was intentional. I wanted to see how the facility was operating when they did not know they were having guests. I wanted the atmosphere to be as much like it would be in everyday life as possible, including whether facility staff would be available to us (potential tenants) as well as the current residents.

On a bright, sunny June day, with a map in hand and a printout of our top contenders (at least from the internet search), we eagerly climbed into the car and began this leg of our journey. Our first stop (well actually more of a slow-down really) found us in front of a sad looking, one story, ugly brown facility. Right there at the curb, Mom said "No." Enough said. We didn't even make it into the lobby. At least for that home, there was no point in even getting out of the car.

Our next stop was a fairly new (within 5 years old) complex that, according to the internet information, had both an independent living area and an assisted living wing. When we first drove up we were very impressed – a gated community with beautiful gardens bursting with flowers and impeccably manicured shrubs. From the parking lot, it looked perfect. The inside followed along the same lines – warm, friendly environment, pleasant and attentive staff, and a nice homey feel.

We met with the sales representative, were given the requisite brochures, and taken on a tour of the facility. Along the way we had an opportunity to ask questions as well as see some of the residents. I was concerned that the population at the facility would be "too geriatric", but was surprised to find a good mix of relatively young and old. There also seemed to be a fairly full program of daily, weekly and monthly activities to keep Mom busy. This place was definitely going to be at the top of our list!

However, as we were looking around the property and asking questions, I inquired as to what the on-going construction was all about out the window to the north of the building. Our tour guide/ sales rep told us that the assisted living portion of the facility was just at the beginning phase of construction. While it was part of the overall plan of the community, it would not be completed and available for occupancy for at least a year. My heart sunk. As I had learned from past experiences, we never know when or how fast, our health can deteriorate. I was not willing to risk that Mom's vision would stay stable at least until the new wing had been built.

We left that community on our list, in the event that we didn't find any other places that were suitable. It was a good (not great) fit for her current needs. It would suffice. But our search continued.

We ran a few errands and stopped for lunch. Our drive continued past a few more facilities, none of which jumped out at us as anything special. Most of the places we put into the "okay" category, for one reason or another (many from the view of the amenities or lack thereof as we'll talk about later).

Finally, a few hours later, when we were getting tired, and essentially done for the day, we drove up to one last complex. Like the others, we looked at the grounds, checked out the surroundings. We went inside and liked what we saw. The sales rep was engaging, kind, and spent as much time with us as we needed (although I'm sure he too wanted to go home). We toured, we asked questions, and we got a feel for the community. It was just what we (Mom and I) wanted. It provided several independent living options (in villas and apartment style units) as well as having a full assisted living wing available too. There were several floor plans to choose from and a variety of financing options. It WAS perfect for what Mom needed and wanted. The sales rep was not pushy or overbearing either – this added greatly to the experience. Mom seemed very pleased, and very impressed. To this day, we say Mom was meant to find that Home.

Finding the right home can be a challenging, overwhelming, and even mind boggling task. To begin in a relatively efficient manner, you need to know, basically, what type or level of care is required. This will help you determine which type of housing is appropriate to meet Mom's needs. Let's start with a review the various kinds of senior living communities.

In most large metropolitan areas, there are several types of senior housing from which to choose. Your goal is to find Mom a facility that provides her with the greatest amount of independence (the least restrictive environment) but with the care and safety that is appropriate for her current health condition. Some facilities may appear more institutional than others. Also, keep in mind, that while you may not WANT to have tile floors, they may be appropriate for the residents in that level of care (carpeting and urinary incontinence do not go together).

The most common types of senior living communities are (note that these terms, and the licensing of the facilities vary from state to state, as each has a particular definition for the type of establishment and service provided): Independent Living, Assisted Living, Memory Care (and other specialized) Units, and Skilled Nursing.

Independent Living is a community environment designed for seniors aged 55 years and older, that are in good health and do not routinely need professional assistance or supervision of their daily activities.

Independent living homes can be organized in neighborhoods of villas (small houses or attached homes), townhomes, and / or condominiums, nearby or adjacent to a common, multi-purpose building. The senior lives in a single unit and is responsible for her own schedule and care. Units may include full sized kitchens, bath tubs, laundry machines, garages and fireplaces. Similar to owning a home or renting an apartment, the senior is free to come and go as she pleases.

In many independent living units, maintenance of the unit, including repairs inside and out, is covered by the complex provider (usually a large company that specializes in service to the senior community).

Additional services such as housekeeping and lawn service are also included. These types of arrangements allow for seniors to be free from worry about maintenance, especially from the safety perspective.

Seniors in this type of home do not require much, if any, medical monitoring or care. However, there are alert buttons and precautions available (and required) in each home. Mom would continue to see her own doctor, scheduling her own appointments. Transportation to and from the appointment may be provided. Likewise, a doctor may come to the facility in lieu of Mom having to travel out.

In the event that an emergency does occur, the independent living complex provider maintains professional on-call medical staff to respond. Standardized safety precautions are in place for each resident, including the extent and location of emergency information for the resident. In some complexes, this simply means a packet of papers with emergency directions and contact names and numbers maintained on the back side of the master bedroom door, and pull cords (or push button) emergency alerts at designated places in each home.

For many independent living communities (aka Retirement Communities), no one under the age of 55 is to live there, although there may be long term visitor arrangements available at the facility for families. Quite frequently these types of homes are marketed to seniors who chose to move in around the time of retirement. The advantages of these complexes are numerous – Mom will not need to move, or not need to move far, if and when she does need extra care; she can build her community of friends at an earlier age when she does still have her faculties; and she can feel more settled into her home while she is still active enough to participate in community events.

Assisted Living environments are appropriate for seniors that are still generally active but need extra assistance with day to day activities to ensure a safe, secure environment. The Assisted Living Federation of America defines Assisted Living as a long-term care option that combines housing, support services and health care, as needed. Seniors in these units (typically condominium or apartment style housing) likely need help managing some or all of the basic daily living tasks such as cooking meals, bathing or dressing themselves, doing laundry, or taking medications without assistance. Assisted living services are customized to ensure that each resident's care is appropriate for meeting the needs of that particular resident.

In Illinois, licensed assisted living communities are required to provide the following services:

> Three meals per day
> Housekeeping services
> Personal laundry and linen services
> 24-hour security and emergency response systems
> Assistance with activities of daily living

According to the *National Survey of Residential Care Facilities*, there are over 31,000 assisted living communities nationwide, serving almost one million seniors. Though it was a relatively new concept 25 years ago, today assisted living is the most preferred and fastest growing long-term care option for seniors.

Memory Care (or other specialized care) Units are available within many long-term care facilities. These specialized areas offer additional protections and services for seniors afflicted with Alzheimer's or dementia. As Alzheimer's disease or dementia progresses, the level of care and assistance a person requires also increases. While you may want to keep your Mom home as long as possible, there will come a time when she may need more care than you can provide.

Individuals with any type of memory loss and confusion, including those afflicted with Alzheimer's, dementia, or other brain injury, are at risk of harming themselves, and others, because their judgment is impaired. Dangers can arise from wandering, hot stoves and even increased falls and balance issues, which are typical for dementia patients. Safety precautions are essential.

In addition, as the disease progresses (and health continues to deteriorate), the patient may not remember how to use common everyday items such as socks and shoes, and toothbrushes, and is at risk for eating foods and other objects that are not suitable for consumption. Additional levels of security and 24 hour supervision are necessary.

A **Skilled Nursing Facility** is what we typically think of when we hear the term "nursing home". This type of facility provides care for patients with chronic conditions for which medical and nursing care are required. Some residents may also be admitted only for short stays of convalescent or rehabilitative care following a hospitalization.

Residents in a skilled nursing facility require continuous nursing care and have significant deficits with the ability to perform the activities of daily living. Skilled nurses and/or nursing assistants are available 24 hours a day.

In a skilled nursing facility, a doctor supervises the senior's care, however several other trained health care professionals are involved in providing the care and will interact with the resident. The care team typically consists of:

Registered nurses for wound care, medication management and monitoring of medical problems;

Physical therapists who will teach Mom how to make her muscles stronger, how to get up and sit down from a chair, toilet, or bed; how to climb steps, keep her balance, and use a walker, cane, or crutches;

Occupational therapists that teach the skills needed to perform everyday tasks at home; and

Speech and language therapists who evaluate and treat problems with swallowing and speech communication.

A skilled nursing facility may also be the appropriate environment for a patient who has a short-term need for rehabilitative services as a result of an injury, stroke, heart attack or other less-protracted ailment. The goal for these individuals is to return home and care for themselves.

Note that some therapy services may also be available at other types of facilities, such as independent living and assisted living, on a per resident basis, as appropriate.

A **Continuing Care Retirement Community**, also known as a CCRC, allows residents the best opportunity to "age in place". These complexes provide a continuum of care including independent living, assisted living, secured Alzheimer's units and skilled nursing care. As a result, CCRCs are also known as "Life Care Communities".

CCRC's can be structured differently, some in a campus style of arrangement. These complexes have several buildings with each level of care provided in a different area of the property. Others centers may have different wings or hallways for care within a fewer number of buildings.

In addition, a CCRC differs from other housing and care options because it typically provides for a written agreement or long-term contract between the resident and the community. The contract lasts for the term of the resident's lifetime. In exchange, the community offers a continuum of housing, services and a health care system.

In some states, CCRCs are regulated developments. However, each part of the community may be subject to separate oversight. For example, independent living oversight might be regulated at a local level, assisted living regulated at the state level, and the skilled nursing units regulated by both state and federal agencies.

As an aside, and even though you, Mom, and her doctors might all agree that a residential facility is best, I will take a minute to share some other non-residential or non-institutional services that might be available in your community. You may consider using these while you are looking for the right residential site, or you may be able to use these to delay a move for a period of time. These alternatives include senior day centers, unconventional senior apartment housing or even senior house-sharing.

Senior day centers (aka Adult Day Care) have become more widely spread in urban areas due to the increasing aging population. According to National Council on Aging, there are 11,400 senior centers serving more than 1 million older Americans every day. Of these participants, 70% are women and with an average age of 75 years old. These individuals, as compared to their peers that do not use such services, have better health, social interaction and life satisfaction. The majority of participants use the center services 1 to 3 days per week, spending about 3 hours there on each visit. The senior centers provide access to many services including meal and nutrition programs; health, fitness and wellness programs; transportation services; public benefits counseling; social and recreational activities; and intergenerational programs.

Senior Apartments may also be available in some locations. These are age-restricted housing units for adults that are able to care for themselves. There is no additional health care service offered by the property owner or manager. The apartments may or may not be regulated by a local housing authority.

Senior House sharing is just as it sounds. Similar to sharing an apartment when you were younger, these arrangements provide a structure for several aging adults to share space and have companionship, while also maintaining a level of autonomy. No additional health care services are provided by the property owners. These arrangements may or may not have live-in managers and may or may not be regulated.

Assessments

The appropriate type of facility for your Mom is going to depend primarily on her cognitive and physical abilities. Although you think you have selected the best, and the most appropriate place, Mom will likely be asked to take a couple of assessments to ensure she is a good match with the facility.

The assessments include medical or health related pieces, in addition to a financial review.

The first assessment is the more important (or irritating, or if it is not explained correctly, the most insensitive and demeaning) test your mother will need to take. You see, while you and she may want to live in a particular community, the facility has the right to determine whether your mother is an appropriate fit for that type of facility – in terms of her cognitive and physical abilities. This in no way should be considered to be condescending – although, it definitely can come across this way.

In particular, the test or questionnaire that is given is a list of routine queries that will satisfy the facility's need to ensure correct placement. The assessment can also be used by the healthcare side of the facility to help create a customized care plan for your mom.

As described by the Hartford Institute for Geriatric Nursing, the functional status of individuals describes the capacity and performance of safe Activities of Daily Living (ADLs) and Instrumental Activities of Daily Living (IADLs). The assessment is a sensitive indicator of health or illness in older adults.

A functional assessment is done, generally by a physician or other healthcare worker, in an effort to gather information and an understanding as to how much ability (or inability) a person has in regards to day to day functioning. Depending on the person, the assessment may be done at a doctor's office or at your own home. It can also be used to identify the resources and support systems that Mom is currently using to function during a typical day. It should be conducted by a third party person so as to relieve the biases that we often come with (our own) which may cast a light on Mom that is much better OR much worse than from an institutional, healthcare perspective.

Keep in mind that follow up assessments are also conducted by healthcare staff to ensure that proper services are being provided.

The initial part of the assessment will cover all areas from self-care to decision making. Areas that are measured include the Activities of Daily Living (ADLs) such as the ability to eat, dress, move (ambulate), bathe, toilet and take care of personal needs.

There will also be an evaluation of the Instrumental Activities of Daily Living (IADLs). These include the more advanced areas of managing finances, administering medications, shopping, doing laundry, performing housekeeping chores, arranging transportation and coordinating medical care.

The absence of the ability to perform any or all of these functions will help the care staff ensure the proper placement in an appropriate type or wing of the facility. For example, if Mom needs assistance with various activities of daily living (toileting, transferring, eating, bathing, dressing), then an assisted living center may be more appropriate than independent living.

Of course if there is memory impairment, then safety precautions are desirable in connection with the stove, walking areas and even trips outside the facility. GPS tracking devices might be needed for each resident to reduce the risk of wandering from safe and controlled areas. Special nutrition and medication management programs may also be appropriate.

If your mom still has a great deal of her cognition, she is likely to be incensed by the questionnaire and the assessment itself. Remind her that it is simply a formality. It is relevant more to those who have lost their functional abilities, and is meant to protect and provide appropriate services for her. It is not meant to treat her like a child.

Upon the completion of the assessment, the doctor will be able to provide you with some guidance as to which type of facility is most appropriate for Mom, from a healthcare perspective.

Financial concerns

Now that we think we have the level of care right, let's talk money. Suffice it to say; moving into a structured living environment is not cheap! As such, a financial assessment will be conducted by the facility. This assessment of Mom's assets is done to ensure that she has enough money not only to buy into the community (if that is required), but also to pay for monthly allotments such as services and amenities that may be included. Think of this in the same manner as when you applied to live in an apartment. The company needs to make sure that you are going to be a credit worthy tenant. Likewise, it will also need to know if Mom is going to be a private pay individual or will be covered by Medicare and Medicaid.

Depending on the particular institution, the facility may ask for Mom's tax returns, Medicare and Medicaid documentation, and any long term care policies. In addition, a financial statement listing all of your Mom's income and assets may be required. CAUTION! Do NOT just believe what Mom has told you in this regard. Remember, she may not be keeping track as closely as she needs to be, thus the reason you are moving her into a supportive living environment. What assets does Mom have? What public benefits is Mom receiving? What is Mom's current monthly income? What are Mom's current monthly expenses?

Data reported on Seniorhomes.com indicates that, in general, assisted living costs are at a national average monthly rate of $3,131. Costs can increase for residents receiving care for Alzheimer's Disease to about $4,267 per month   (2009 data). In the state of Illinois, the average cost for assisted living is $4,057 per month.

As detailed at APlaceforMom.com, the costs for senior housing vary based on the type of facility and the level of care that is needed.

Type of Facility	Approx. Cost per Month
Independent Living	$1500-$3500
Assisted Living	$2500-$4000
Skilled Nursing	$4000 -$8000

Other differences in cost relate to the amount and type of services provided, such as:

Included meals per day
Medication management
Personal care support services
Mobility assistance services
Alzheimer's / Dementia care
On-site nurses
Transportation
Incontinence Care
Housekeeping

Don't be distressed though. There are several payment options, including those listed below. Your mom may be able to use a combination of these to cover the costs. Also, keep in mind that there is a possibility that some of the costs may be treated as medical expenses on her tax return (consult with your tax accountant for more detail on these).

Private Funds
Long Term Care Insurance
Senior Living Line of Credit
Medicaid
Medicare
Supplemental Security Income
Veteran's Benefits

As a note, in Illinois, the term "supportive living facility" refers to homes similar to assisted living establishments that are designed to provide care to low-income adults.

As detailed on Medicare.gov, most people begin to pay for long term care with private funds. When (if) these funds are depleted, the resident may then qualify for Medicaid.

Private Funding includes essentially all funds that are not public benefits – therefore, long term care insurance, individual savings and investments.

As for Medicaid, it can provide federal health-care assistance to low-income Americans. It is the biggest payer for room, board, nursing care, and social activities in nursing homes. Many, but not all, states now cover some assisted living services under their Medicaid programs; however, these vary widely in terms of eligibility requirements, and dollar amounts of coverage. The Senior Assisted Housing Waiver provides eligible low-income adults a choice of receiving senior living care services in a community-based setting rather than in a nursing facility.

Do not confuse Medicaid with Medicare. With respect to Medicare: neither Medicare Parts A nor B offer coverage for comprehensive ongoing long-term care.

Medicare A (hospital insurance) may cover costs for a semiprivate room, meals, nursing and rehab services, medications, and medical supplies in a skilled nursing facility for the first 100 days after being released from hospitalization for an acute illness or injury. It never covers a private room nor services in an assisted living residence. (Medicare B only offers reimbursement for covered services you receive from a doctor.)

Housing and Veterans Subsidies: Seniors with annual incomes under $12,000 may qualify for U.S. Department of Housing and Urban Development 202 and Section 8 senior housing, which provide rent subsidies that can help pay for the room-and-board portion of both independent living and assisted living environments. The Department of Veterans Affairs also provides some skilled and intermediate-level care to veterans in its own residences, depending on space availability.

The long term care facility will help you in coordinating payments from a public benefit. However, your mother (or you as her personal representative or Power of Attorney) will need to apply for the benefit itself.

Depending on the facility, Mom may only need to pay a monthly "rent" which would cover room and board. In these instances Mom (or more likely you or her Power of Attorney) will receive a monthly invoice which includes Room, Board (meals), prescription medications, therapies, etc. Additional services such as haircuts, telephone, etc. may be included or billed separately. Most assisted living, memory care and skilled nursing facilities charge a monthly "rent".

Other facilities, usually independent living units and CCRC's, have "buy in" programs which require a larger initial investment, plus some monthly allotments. This arrangement is similar to actually buying a condominium or house. In these circumstances, a portion of the initial investment (ranging from 70-95%) is recovered by Mom's estate upon her death or upon re-sale of the unit. Monthly allotments are also made to cover service fees such as meal plans, cable television, phone service, etc. In connection with this financing option, mortgage loans may also be available.

With some independent living and CCRC facilities, the capital investment paid by Mom can also be used to pay down expenses in the event that Mom outlives her assets. Thus, these facilities have earned the term "life care facilities". Be sure to inquire about the possibility of this type of payment plan while speaking with the sales representative.

Specific costs of each type of facility may also vary based on the type of residence (independent living vs. assisted living), size of the unit or apartment, number of tenants (perhaps Mom and Dad will be moving in together?), and the types of services needed. As you can imagine, the more services (or more specialized types of service), the higher the cost. Therefore, you can expect that skilled nursing would cost more than assisted living, etc.

Now you know some of the basics to the types of housing options, the assessments for placement and the finances. But you are not done yet! A few more reviews can be done (some from the convenience of your desk) before you decide on the perfect home for Mom.

Start with a general Google search of the facility you have in mind. See if any information comes up, other than that published directly by the facility.

Check with your local Better Business Bureau to see if any complaints or complements have been received on your chosen homes.

You can also look into the licensing of the facility by searching http://www.aging.state.il.us/ccir/1welcomeintro.htm for the state of Illinois. For other states, APlaceForMom.com has a portal at http://www.aplaceformom.com/assisted-living-state-licensing.

If you are still uncertain, you can also review state and federal court actions against the facility.

Some other things to consider when searching out a facility include:

How long has the corporation been in business?

Who manages the corporation?

Who manages the individual facility in which Mom may live?

Is the facility part of a larger corporation?

If the facility or its governing corporation, has not been in existence for very long (at least 5 years), then you want to conduct additional reviews or due diligence.

Inquire as to who is managing the property operationally and financially.

Who is in charge of the provision of services?

Who is in charge of the financial operations?

Is there a board of directors that they report to?

What experience does each of the people on the Board have in running a geriatric living center? A health care facility?

Do the Board members and their family members live in the facility?

Does the company's website provide detailed information about the facility and who is running it?

Some other questions to ask while on your tour of the community:

Can you tour the entire facility?

Are they open about the pricing structures? Are there alternatives to the pricing (or one simple structure for everyone?) or is it a Life-care situation where regardless of the level of care needed they will NOT kick Mom out?

How are emergencies handled?

How does Mom call for help? Does she wear a monitor? Need to phone someone? Push a button?

What is the typical response to an emergency? Who responds? What is the response time? How long after the emergency will you be contacted?

Is a particular hospital used for medical emergencies? Is it always this hospital?

Is a Registered Nurse on site at all times?

How does the facility maintain the resident's emergency information (on the back of the bedroom door)? Is it systematic in all units?

Something for you to know, that should give you and Mom some peace of mind, is that each facility has its own system for daily well-being checks. These are precautionary overt actions taken by each resident. The purpose is to ensure the resident's safety and security. It may be as simple as a sign or switch on the door to the unit; a special button to push each day or a phone call to make.

Please remind Mom that this is not overbearing or childish. ANYONE can slip and fall. ANYONE can need assistance. Find out what the procedure is for Mom to follow. Also, find out what happens if she does not do what is required (either because she forgot, or because she has had an event).

A few more things for you and Mom to consider:

Are your Mom's doctors already affiliated with the hospital used by the facility? Will she need to get new doctors?

What is the geographic distance from:

Your home
Family friends
Church
Grocery stores and shopping malls
Airport

Yours and your Mom's knowledge of these things will relieve a lot of stress and anxiety for both of you.

Location in the country may or may not matter to you or to Mom. However, there are some benefits to living in other states (whether you are elderly or not) such as state taxes, access to specialty services, and eldercare community events. These may or may not make a difference to you and to Mom when you're out on your hunt.

Answers to many of the questions you might have will be dependent upon the stage of life Mom is in, as well as how involved you are with your Mom's care. The more involved you are, the less she may need outside support. Likewise, the more outside (and professional) care that is offered, the less burden there is on family.

My recommendation to you is to take a tour of a couple of facilities BEFORE you take Mom out to visit them. It's best for YOU to get over the sticker shock – and facility shock – so that it doesn't show on your face when you're with Mom.

We're not completely done with this leg of our journey, though we've made some good progress. Also on this route we must consider the amenities for Mom's new home. Just around the bend we'll see the possibilities and consider what is necessary versus what are truly "extras", some worth every penny!

Steps to Take

1. Determine which level of care is most appropriate for Mom.

2. Determine which housing type is most appropriate for Mom.

3. Do a financial analysis for your mom.

4. Obtain (create) a list of possible homes in the geographic location of choice.

5. Narrow down list of homes by care level and financial constraints.

6. Review choices available and re-assess both location and cost, if needed. Do NOT diminish Mom's level of care.

7. Pick the most promising five homes to tour.

8. Tour each of the five facilities within a short period of time (all within one month, if possible). Ask similar questions at each so that you can compare. (We'll be discussing amenities in the next chapter so don't make any decisions yet!) Take notes on each (after a few, they all begin to look the same).

9. Review your choices against the care that is offered. Does it fit what Mom needs?

10. Conduct a due diligence review of the financial aspects of the facility. Include searches of the Better Business Bureau, court filings, state licensing departments, etc.

11. Conduct a due diligence review of the service levels (including level of care) of the facility. Include reference checks with current and former residents (and/or their families).

Questions for Thought

1. What type of community structure would Mom like to live in?

2. What level of care does Mom really need?

3. What emergency support assistance will you need? Or are you the only contact person?

4. Is a single home (duplex, villa, townhome) too much house for her to maintain? What about in winter months? In summer months?

5. Is an apartment/ condo style living arrangement more appropriate to meet her needs (and not be too big for her)?

6. What type of support services do you think Mom needs?

7. Can Mom perform the activities of daily living?

8. Can Mom perform the instrumental activities of daily living?

9. Financially, what can Mom afford? Are other sources of income available?

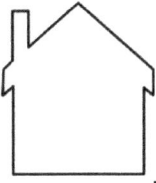

Chapter 4

It's All About The Amenities

The amenities: those little extras that make all the difference. The pleasures of life, some of which we've become so accustomed that they are no longer indulgences but are now requirements! You know what I'm talking about. For me it's an elevator in a tall building (actually anything over 3 floors), bright rooms with lots of windows, and a clean, warm, inviting entry way.

When I travel I look for hotels that have the amenities that I want. Why not? I'm the one who gets to choose where I'm staying. Standard in most rooms are the hair dryer and coffee maker. However my "Must Have" list also includes a fitness center on the premises (a pool puts it into the luxury category!), free continental breakfast, and free Wi-Fi. The rest of the options are just that, options – extras, perks, benefits of that particular hotel.

The same is true when you are looking for a new house. What <u>must</u> you have? What would you like? And what, if money, location or design is a barrier, do you think you could probably live without? Do you have your list in mind?

Now let's look on the flip side. It's almost just as important to know what is a definite "NO!" when it comes to a new place. A NO! could be anything from small children to pets to too big of a complex. It might also mean location or price or even a particular floor plan. I like to call these "Deal Breakers".

Ideally, you will find a house that has a lot (or ALL!) of the amenities you want, with none of the Deal Breakers. (In your dreams, you may also get it for a fantastic price!) Although, at the end of the day (or the search in this case), your list of Must Haves and your list of Deal Breakers may need to be revised.   You might not be able to get the best of both worlds.

Mom's new house, just like yours, should be a mixture of the necessities and the perks, with none (or as few as possible) of the Deal Breakers. Keep looking for places that meet her needs and offer what she really wants. If you are lucky enough to live in a larger metropolitan area, then you should have plenty from which to choose. In this search however, compromise is key - unless you have a facility built especially for her!

My mom's Must Haves included plenty of cabinets and cupboards in the kitchen, big closets, a washer and dryer in her apartment, and a den (or small second bedroom). We were fortunate to find several facilities that granted Mom her wishes. She did, however, have to concede on the bathtub, a balcony and a fireplace.

Of course it wasn't just as easy as that. When we actually found the facility and the floor plan that matched Mom's desires, we hit a bump in the road. There was no availability. We had a choice: pick a new unit that did not have all the features Mom wanted OR wait until her perfect match became vacant. Since she *did* have the luxury of time, we decided to wait. Putting a reasonable deposit down to secure the next opening, we were able to finally buy the unit in November (remember, our on-site search began in June!). Mom was thrilled.

One of the other amenities that Mom was fortunate to gain as a result of moving into this particular place was a Chapel. And better yet, the Chapel connected via hallways to her complex. She was less than 3 minutes' walk from church. The Chapel's high, ornately painted ceilings, beautiful statues and pictures, and crucifix are all amazing.   I immediately felt a sense of peace when I walked in, and Mom did too. Mom says the Chapel is what really sold her on the facility. She has been going to daily Mass for several years, and knowing that she would be able to continue this pattern was comforting for me too.

The amenities that Mom fell in love with did not stop there. She wanted a place that had a variety of activities, including field trips, classes and gatherings. Once again, she was in luck. The activity schedule was posted in the reception area and we could see while on our tour just how many choices she would have to make. A quick view at the month's events showed concerts, plays, painting class and bible study, just to name a few. Mom was pleased that the selection went beyond just Bingo and Pinochle.

As Mom describes her Home now, she refers to it as a "resort". The Piazza (common living room area) and other sitting areas are warmly decorated and inviting. The Bistro has a lovely outdoor seating area and there is a Lounge off to the side of the dining room. Heck, if I were over age 55, I'd live there!

Now, it's your turn. Where do you begin? Start at the most practical and important point: Ask Mom! Remember, you already have her agreement, at least to the concept, and you've narrowed down the universe to the appropriate type of facility. Now let's try to find that perfect fit with the amenities that are offered and what Mom is picturing as her new home.

Amenities can fall into three categories: those included in the price, those routine items with an extra monthly charge, and those that are limited one-time events. Ask the sales representative which of the amenities that Mom wants falls into each of these groups. The facility should be able to provide you with a list for each category.

Keep in mind the type of institution that you are in, and the level of care and safety that is needed for those particular types of residents. There will obviously be more possibilities and alternatives for the independent living groups than for a Memory Care wing. Still each type of location should provide those services and extras that will keep the resident's engaged in social, intellectual, emotional and physical activities.

Items typically included in the price of the monthly rental (or buy-in), will depend on the type of facility into which Mom is moving. These can include formal dining room service, housecleaning, and laundry service, certain activities such as card games and movie night, and social entertainment. Sometimes even health lectures and services (blood pressure checks, etc.) are provided to the group.

Things that are usually extra monthly charges include internet access, cable TV, and long-distance phone plans.

Other limited one-time items include trips to plays, educational classes (like Mom's Bible study) and even wine tasting! These activities are available to those who wish to participate, and are willing to pay the additional cost. For the off-campus activities, transportation is also provided.

Speaking of transportation, as you are reviewing the amenities offered, find out the extent of the transport service available. Most care facilities offer shuttle service to nearby shopping, doctor offices, etc. Mom may or may not also be able to have the van take her on other personal trips.

As you and Mom take a tour of any facility, think about what might meet her needs. Pay attention to her reaction as you walk through the lobby, as you review the activities list, as you stroll through the gardens. What perks her up? What is she indifferent to? Is the Home decorated? Is it adorned in a style that suits your Mom's taste?

Remember, this is Mom's new home, not yours. Put yourself in her shoes – what activities does she like and will she do (my mom thought a pool would be nice, but honestly, I had to question whether she would really ever use it).

Listed below are some of the amenities that can be found at various senior living communities. Remember, depending on the facility, and the type of care level that is appropriate, some of these may not be provided.

Additional services and areas at the community:

Fitness room
Beauty Salon
Bank
Gift shop
Garden spots
Swimming pool
Formal Dining Room
Bistro / Café
Bar / Lounge
Storage units
Church / Chapel
Outdoor patio
Art Studio
Doctor visits on-site
Library
Gated Community
Outdoor walking paths and gardens
Trash disposal on each floor
Party rooms for private gatherings
Lawn care
Emergency response buttons

Activities at the community:

> Card games
> Brain games
> Bingo
> Movie nights
> Arts and Crafts
> Entertainment – singers, musicians, etc.
> Exercise classes
> Blood pressure clinic
> Educational seminars and lectures

Outings available:

> Concerts
> Plays
> Botanical Gardens/ parks
> Local sporting events
> Shopping trips

Items within Mom's room / apartment:

> Bed
> TV
> DVD player
> Dresser
> Washer and dryer
> Bathroom
> Bath tub
> Second bathroom
> Second bedroom
> Eat in kitchen / kitchenette
> Cleaning service
> Cable TV
> Internet connection

Patio or Balcony
Maintenance on appliances
Utilities included – electric, water
Telephone
Temperature controls

Finally, don't forget some of the larger items that might make Mom's stay more comfortable to her: size of the complex, pets permissible, and a covered parking garage.

Look for those amenities which are affordable, but also provide Mom with the greatest opportunity to be as independent and self-sufficient as she can be. Be sure to select those amenities which are going to accommodate and support Mom's specific needs.

Almost every unit will have features that appear to be handicap accessible. Other items may seem to be extras, but are actually required (depending on the facility):

Large doorways
Extra lighting
Wide hallways
Required name tags
Wellness checks
Hand rails in bathrooms

Further yet, some amenities may not be specifically available at the facility, but are located in the neighborhood or through connections with the complex. Be sure to inquire if there is transportation available. Will the facility help Mom to gain access to these?

Churches
Malls
Dry cleaners
Laundry service (even if it is an extra charge)

Cooking / meals
Meals delivered to room
Bringing guests to dinner

Ask, too, if additional services or maintenance can be done for Mom inside her unit. Find out if she can personalize the room or apartment. Her favorite colors, wall hangings, pictures and even furniture will help her settle into her new place quicker and easier. Find out if there are services available to fix computers, for repair of appliances or even something as simple as changing light bulbs.

Find out if there are any restrictions for the facility, such as no pets and no children overnight. Also see if there is a limitation on decorations that can be displayed. For some more protected wings, special visitation hours may be enforced.

Don't be surprised if the facility does tell you 'No" to your request for certain items. For safety reasons, for your Mom, as well as other residents, it may not be appropriate to have some of the amenities that Mom is used to.   There will likely be no floor rugs (tripping hazard), no swimming pool (liability), no fireplaces (fire hazard), no gas stoves (fire hazard), and no bathtubs (fall hazard). Depending on the type of facility, especially Memory Care wings, there will also be no kitchens (or only some appliances but nothing such as toasters or stoves/ovens), and no in-unit laundry machines.

In many complexes that include Independent living houses, you may find an additional perk. There may be extra units available that families can use when coming to visit Mom. These types of arrangements allow visitors to rent out the unit for a certain number of days at a relatively inexpensive rate, similar to a hotel. Dining room privileges may or may not be included in the rate.

Finally, there are other items which are not amenities, but that are simply stand objects in any institutional residential setting.   These include fire extinguishers, smoke detectors and sprinklers, defibrillators and security.

As you can see, the list of choices is almost endless. Be sure that Mom gets to choose at least some of her favorite activities, and features for her room – to the extent that each is appropriate for her care level (sorry, there will be no sky diving or zip-lining on this trip).

Steps to Take

1. Discuss with Mom which amenities are important to her.

2. Rank the level of importance for the amenities – MUST haves, wants, definite NO's.

3. Determine what is already included in the price (will the price go down, if Mom doesn't use the amenity? Will the price go up, if she does want the amenity – cable TV, Wi-Fi-, long distance phone package?)

4. Review the choices of homes already identified and compare the amenities included.

5. Determine if other desired amenities are possible to obtain, as separate line items, versus being included in the base cost of the potential home choices (cable tv, internet, telephone, etc.)

6. Determine if any of the homes contain the definite NO's from the list. Eliminate those homes from your short list of choices. (Note – if this eliminates all the homes, then you need to re-evaluate the "definite NO" list and not be so critically harsh).

7. For the desired additional amenities, are they cost comparative to bundle together versus buying each separately (if they can be added separately)?

8. When touring each possible home, make a list of the amenities and assign a "value" to each one. Then compare and re-assess.

One home might be perfect, except for a missing balcony. Decide then if it is really needed.

9. Inquire as to who will perform maintenance on the amenities.

Questions for Thought

1. What amenities are important *to Mom* to have in her new home?

2. What amenities does Mom want to pay for – whether for a few months, years or forever?

3. Do you have to ask permission prior to making changes to the apartment – walls painted, different flooring, pictures hung, draperies/blinds, etc.?

4. Who will handle repairs of major interior items – sink, refrigerator, plumbing, heating/air conditioning, laundry machines, if the maintenance of these items is not provided?

5. Who handles small odd job repairs (i.e. light bulbs changed)?

6. Who will do the cleaning, if the service is not provided?

7. What other activities and errands will you need to do for Mom, if it is not available as a service or amenity?

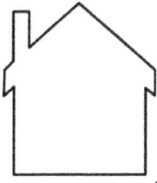

Chapter 5

Downsizing

The childhood photos, the macaroni necklaces, the handmade Christmas ornaments . . . the art project from 2nd grade. These old, tattered relics are the things that moms keep. The things they treasure; the things you will need to help clean out.

At this point in our lives, most of us have moved at least a time or two. So has Mom. But this time is different. This time, Mom is moving away from a home where memories were made, where challenges were overcome, and where the family spent time 'as a family'. All that she will have left are the memories, of the blessings she shared, the wounds she helped heal, of the milestones and the heartaches, of the rites of passage. The memories of life.

This time is not completely unlike when we, as young adults, finally decided to fly the coup; to "grow up" and move out into the world, into our own house or apartment. Back then, we had to decide whether to take with us every stuffed animal, every high school sports trophy and every prom picture. The souvenirs of our childhood: the board games and toys, the high school yearbooks and the letter jackets.

Now, its Mom's turn. As you help her sort through the years and years of "stuff" that has collected, each piece brings back a flood of memories of the day, the time, maybe even the event at which it was received. You see, moms like to keep those small treasures – the outfit you wore home from the hospital, your first swim suit, the list goes on. Whatever held precious memories in her heart, you can be assured she will have some keepsake from the moment. Come to think of it, I am doing the same thing!

I've had my share of cleaning out houses. First was my Grandma and Grandpas. After Grandma died, I went to stay with Grandpa for a couple of weeks to help him "sort out" some of Grandma's old things and take them to donation. For the first week of that trip, I sat next to Grandpa listening to stories of his days with Grandma- the trips they took, the parties they attended, and the love and friendship which they shared. When I would gently ask Grandpa if he was ready to clean out Grandma's closet, his response was brief, a whispered "Let's do it later next week." By the end of my two week visit, we had not been separated from any of Grandma's things. But I would never have said the trip was unproductive. Those times that I spent with Grandpa are now my blessed memories, and they gave me a glimpse into the unique and powerful love that Grandma and Grandpa shared.

The day did come, though, only a couple of years later, for me to clean out Grandma and Grandpa's house completely. After Grandpa too had passed away, I handled the "business end" of packing up the memories, the antiques and the heirlooms. My mom and I sorted through the treasures, setting aside those things we knew we wanted to keep. After that, we made several trips to the Salvation Army, the car loaded with clothes, dishes, and small appliances. Finally, I had to call the garbage company. No joke – I literally got a dumpster – AND had it emptied 3 times! Grandma and Grandpa had lived in that house for over 50 years. There was simply a lot of "stuff"!

So now, you, the business minded adult child that you are, need to remind yourself that for Mom to shuffle through the boxes upon boxes of YOUR memories may take more than just an hour or two. In addition to your belongings (which you may finally need to take back to your own house), Mom has her own assortment of knick knacks that she collected over the years from family, vacations, trips to museums, zoos or state parks.   Of course there are the gifts that others have sent her too– pictures from their trips, vacations and outings. Each item represents a story, a memory, a gift to be remembered.

YOUR childhood stuff, your Mom's childhood stuff, the family knick knacks ---and that's just the beginning. There's also the furniture, the clothes, and the shoes (yes, they are a category of their own).

Where do you begin? Get rid of the easy things first – old clothes that no longer fit or that have too many stains to even count, worn out plastic containers that have no matching lids (the biggest mess in my mom's house!), old bed sheets, etc. Once you feel like you have made some progress, then move on to the larger projects.

If you are in the same situation that I was, Mom is moving from a house of 4-5 rooms full of beds, couches, tables and chairs. Not to mention, downsizing from the full service kitchen ware (PLUS the special china that was only used once or twice a year), the books, and the photo albums. Think before you act.

A new house, whether it's one room or two, might even require new furniture, built to fit the space. It's hard to put a king size bed into most one bedroom apartments.   And depending on the type of facility, a bed may not be something that is brought along anyway. Before you get rid of all of it, though, check to see if she can take any of the bigger pieces with her to her new home. It might be that only *some* of the furniture can go. Whatever you can take though is well worth it. Having parts of her old house with her will help to ease the transition.

On to the clothes closet. Before you simply donate it all or conversely, keep every last sweater, consider where Mom is moving. What is the type of climate? Is it colder? Warmer? What type of social atmosphere is at her new house? Will she need to "dress" for dinner? Are jeans okay? Will she need a bathrobe? As you are helping her go through her things, have a little fun. Remember, there are probably memories mixed in with the clothes too.

Be warned that if Mom is helping you, then you may need to make some "executive" decisions. Mom will probably want to keep everything. But can you find the matching gloves? Or are they with the half dozen mismatched socks behind the dryer? Are the boxy, oversized, shoulder-padded blazers still in style? And seriously, how many night gowns does one woman need? Make sure she is taking the appropriate clothing for her new environment, plus a few of the things she just can't seem to part with (wink, wink). (Sigh) Just don't be too quick to judge. Many of these outfits were bought for a special reason too.

Now, the shoes. I have put shoes into their own category for one specific reason. Women love shoes! At least everyone I know does. It's rare to find a woman's closet with fewer than 10 pairs of shoes. But consider this, does Mom really need even that many now? When was the last time Mom wore high heels? If you can't remember, then why oh why does she still have ½ of a closet full of them!? My suggestion would be to keep a few flat loafers, some slippers and perhaps one or two pairs of low heeled shoes for more formal occasions. Nevertheless, good luck trying to get her to part with any more than necessary.

While you are going through her things, think too about any heirlooms that she may have kept from previous generations. And what about Mom's own things that she might want to pass down? Her wedding dress? Her jewelry? This is a great time to talk about to who and where these small (or large) mementos will go.

I want to make a special note about jewelry. I know it's small and delicate. And that is precisely the point – it's small and delicate. Depending on Mom's ailments, is she still able to put on the necklace and earrings, with or without assistance? And not to say that every home will be like this, but sometimes small things do end up "missing". Perhaps it's time to make these pieces family heirlooms.

Mom may still be reluctant to part with her things. Don't worry. You and I (and Mom) know that not everything can be kept either. It's always possible to get a storage unit to keep some of her things until she is ready to let them go. In fact, taking a slower pace, sorting out the house and her things in phases, may help to minimize the trauma of disposing of a life time of collections.

I have found that if Mom still has her mental faculties (and only for a physical reason does she need to move), she is going to stall. She is going to require your guidance and your assistance to get the job done. Remember, though, if she had all her faculties, both mental and physical, she would not need to move.

If Mom is not yet in a situation where she must move, or if she is contemplating the change for several months ahead, then that is even better. You can start now anyway. Downsize one day, or one room, at a time.

Either way, I've found that going through the process of downsizing, especially for this reason (due to a decline in health), is a traumatic experience for Mom. She may be thinking that she has to get rid of memories so to speak – or at least the physical reminders of them. It is best not to set too strict of a time line to sorting and divesting of these goods. If you do, you only cause resentment, anger and depression. Remember, the reason for the move is that Mom can no longer live in her current home anymore – psychologically (even if not physically) that means she's aging – that's a hard thing to accept.

Let time take its course. Be there with her to sort through the treasures, listen to the stories, laugh about the silly memories and cry about the sad remembrances. Don't, under any circumstances, throw out things she is not ready to throw out. There will be other opportunities to purge the "extras" in her life. During the big downsizing is not always the right time.

Along with the downsizing, you can also begin to think about packing. In fact, these two steps can go hand in hand – even if you don't anticipate moving for several weeks. Once you and Mom have decided that its time for her to move, start "purging" and packing her current home.

Consider what might need to be "recycled" BEFORE you list the house. Talk to the real estate agent to see if there are items which might be packed or donated to make the house "show" better. These might be the easiest things to start with.

If the house is already listed for sale when your downsizing project begins, let the realtor know if you are not going to be able to finish a particular project (i.e. sorting of dozens of family photographs). Your endeavor to clean and sort may make the house appear messy and cluttered to prospective buyers. The realtor can let the new prospective buyers know that this is merely a temporary issue.

On a related note, take a hard look at the house from the point of cleanliness. Do any rooms look as if they need a "heavy" or significant amount of cleaning? Be sure to check the cabinets and shelves too, especially in the kitchen. Quite frequently as people are aging, their "version" of a clean house differs from yours and mine. Mom likely has not cleaned the same way that a cleaning company would or maintained the house in such a manner that it would fetch a good price. Even clutter in rooms can make the house appear to be 'unkept and uncared for'. Downsize the knick knacks, replace or throw out the broken items.

Mom may be reluctant to put the house on the market, mentioning that it "needs to be cleaned out first" or that it "needs some knick knacks packed up" before it can be listed. If pressed, she may even go so far as to shout, "I'll get to it. Don't rush me!"

Don't fret too much. She does make sense, in a way. But her delay tactics are more likely being done a result of her own preference (consciously or not) to stall the move. The things in the house still hold memories. Packing (or throwing) them away can be difficult and emotional.

I'm sure she will never admit to purposely trying to postpone the inevitable. But consider how her progress is going on its own, without your help. Has she been "too busy" to work on it? Has she simply not made any progress in sorting through her things? She may not even realize how little she has actually done until it's been pointed out.

Gently remind her of the reason for the downsizing, focusing on the positive aspects of cleaning out unneeded items. With the continued poverty and despair in today's society, surely someone will be able to use Mom's surplus items.

Be patient though. Control your own emotions and eagerness to simply "get the house cleaned out and packed". Don't be harsh with Mom. This is a highly emotional time as she realizes that her life is changing, and not necessarily for the better. Remind her that she will still have her memories, even if she does not have all the material possessions that came along with them. Each memory can still hold the joy, the love and the smiles.

Steps to Take

1. Set aside time to help Mom clean out her house – preferably a couple of hours per day over several days.

2. If there is time, downsize first, then later pack into boxes.

3. Check with the new facility to see if there are any restrictions on what can be brought in – plants, furniture, etc.

4. Make a quick timeline or deadline in which downsizing needs to occur. Left open-ended, it just might not ever get done.

5. If selecting items for donation is too difficult collectively, then go through one room at a time, selecting only a few things. You may then need to make several passes through each room to cull down the furniture, trinkets, etc.

6. Work with Mom to downsize. Listen to her stories and memories about the items you find. Take the time to reminisce.

7. If Mom wants to keep multiple sets of the same thing, let her keep one to use, then one for a backup (which will be stored in a storage locker). The rest are better used by others who need them.

8. As you downsize the kitchen, go through the cabinets and refrigerator and throw out all expired perishable items. She can buy new, if she needs them at her new home.

9. Do not judge what Mom decides to keep, as long as it's within reason.

10. Put the donations into the car or charity box as soon as possible (out of sight, out of mind), then drop them off or call for pick up before the end of the day.

11. Encourage Mom to keep only those things that will fit into her new lifestyle.

12. Don't stress if she seems to be keeping too much. You can also donate more after the move if it doesn't fit into the new living environment.

13. Sort children's childhood reminders (art projects, school grades, yearbooks, first teddy bears, pictures) into separate boxes per child and send to each child (Mom no longer needs to keep these).

14. Start packing in a system – knick knacks first, then kitchen, bath, clothes, etc. OR pack room by room. This will depend on the urgency in which you need to downsize and pack – your time commitment versus Mom's need to move.

15. Label the boxes carefully – some items may be able to go right into storage at the new house (precious mementos or china which she does not want to get rid of).

Questions for Thought

1. Consider Mom's new surrounding and lifestyle when deciding what she will keep (climate, cooking needs, cleaning supplies, etc.).

2. Who will help Mom downsize – one person or the whole family?

3. Do you have the time to do the downsizing over a period of weeks or even months?

4. Will Mom downsize on her own, without some help or support of family?

5. Does Mom have friends that might help her downsize, instead of you?

6. Are there family heirlooms which might be passed down now?

7. Consider donation versus a garage sale, for items no longer needed or wanted?

8. Are there any significant items which might be sold instead of donated (i.e. newer furniture, car)?

9. Consider selling the furniture with the house instead of moving it.

10. Does Mom need to keep ALL of the dinnerware, glasses and mugs, or can some be donated? If she wants to keep it all, is she willing to put some into storage?

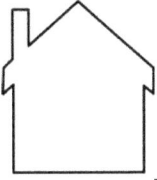

Chapter 6

The Big Day

My advice to you: Bring Kleenex!

Even if it seems that Mom should be ready for this, she won't be. Up to this point, it's all been preparation. Kind of like "in theory" she will move. Nothing, including the downsizing part, is as REAL as the actual move out of the old and into the new.

For most, this isn't the first move in a lifetime, but it may be the last. There is a finality to it. An emotional impact that is not only hard to describe, but even harder to accept. It comes with hesitation, worry and reluctance; it comes with grief and sadness.

You will ask yourself, "Am I doing the right thing for Mom?"

Mom will ask herself, "Am I doing the right thing?"

Neither of you want to be dramatic about this move, but it IS life changing. Once on this road, you will never turn back.

Emotions are high. Time is short. There is so much to do before and while the movers are here. But you must keep your cool, so as not to further upset Mom.

My mom's move still replays in my head like a slow motion picture. Although she still has her cognitive ability, she was silent, almost as if she were in shock, at the actual process of the move. Mom was with me on the day I called the moving company to line up services. She was there the day the lead mover came to assess the bevy of boxes and furniture to pack into the truck. She was there when the moving truck arrived and the crew jumped out eager and ready to begin their task. She was there – but yet she was frozen in time. With a Kleenex in her hand, and a somber expression on her face, she just stood. In the center of the empty living room, she stood immobile, except for the gentle tears rolling down her cheeks.

This was the first house Mom had bought completely on her own. It had been her "home" for the past 13 years. She had caringly decorated it the way she wanted, wisely picked out each piece of furniture, and filled it full of the love and memories that only a Mom can do. And now she had to leave it.

We watched as the moving men loaded the last of the cartons into the back end of the truck and shut the doors. I signed off on the paperwork, confirming the new address, our phone numbers and our expected arrival time. Mom didn't say a word.

My heart went out to her. Yet, I knew we were making the right decision. Time heals all wounds. This too would be okay. . . eventually.

More advice: think business-like. For just these few hours, try to keep emotion out of it. Have your pad of paper. Have your pen. Jot down things as you think of them, lest you forget in all the fuss. Even though it is Mom that is actually moving, due to her physical and/or cognitive issues, you need to treat this move as if it is you that is changing houses. You (or whoever you and Mom have appointed) will need to ensure that all the tasks and all the paperwork are done. This includes everything from hiring movers, giving the movers both addresses, arranging for use of the loading dock at the new facility, and of course payment and paper signing for the movers and at the new home.

Logistically speaking, think orderly - but backwards. Start by getting a move IN date from Mom's new place and schedule use of the loading dock. Find out the parameters and feasibility of using other doors or access points if you are bringing in additional items (such as suitcases, plants, etc.) from your car. Next, hire movers that can bring the van and the muscle power to load the truck. Make arrangements for the movers to come to Mom's soon-to-be old house to move OUT, with sufficient time for you (and them) to then travel to the new place and unload at your designated time. Now finish packing the boxes (and continue to downsize if that is still an option). Don't forget to leave out one suitcase of essential clothes for Mom, along with her toiletries. As you know, the unpacking side of a move can take quite a bit of time too. And you will want to make sure Mom is as comfortable as she can be during the entire process.

Now, let's discuss more specific pointers for along the way. First, moving out. Before the moving van is even in the driveway, your head will be swimming with a million questions and thoughts. Did I order the right size truck? Are we taking everything we need? I sure hope we didn't throw out things that Mom still might want. And you'll answer yourself too: "It's too late now, the truck is here."

Make a list of the "moving out" jobs that need to be taken care of at Mom's old house:

> Forward the mail (decide who will pay the bills if it's not Mom; you may want the bills to go to her Power of Attorney instead)
> Cancel utilities – electric, gas, phone, garbage, water
> Cancel cable TV and return the cable box
> Discontinue lawn service

If the house has not been sold yet, then you may need to continue with utilities, lawn service, etc. until the new owner has possession. Remember; think of it just like it is your own house.

Check in with the movers as they are loading the truck. Although they are professionals, you may need to give them guidance on what furniture will end up in which room of the new house. When they have finished loading the truck, sign off on the loading end paperwork. Confirm delivery again, and double check the address and loading dock times. Be sure to give the movers your cell phone number too just in case any issues arise.

On your way out the door for the last time, give Mom another few minutes to be with her house. Don't push her, but don't let her wallow too long either. Be quiet. Be patient.

Once the final goodbyes to the house are done, you and Mom can slide into the car. Pause and take a deep breath. You are ready to move forward on this journey. Remind yourself, and Mom, that you are doing the right thing. Everything is going to work out fine.

Whether it's a just a few miles down the road or several hours away, the journey to the new home can seem endless. Mom may want to talk, or she may want silence. Try engaging her in a light hearted discussion about her new upcoming environment. This may keep the mood light and thinking positively. Be cautious though. If she doesn't want to talk, don't force it. Sometimes the best we can do is simply just "be" with a person. Let her actions and emotions drive this part of the trip.

Upon arriving at Mom's new home, your heart may still be filled with anxiety. Your body is functioning just fine, but your mind is funneling a whirlwind of feelings. Say loudly enough for both of you to accept, "We're here, Mom. Your new home."

Be cheerful. Be happy. She's moving on to another adventure, another phase of her life. And you are right there beside her to see that she takes her first step (figuratively speaking) without worry or fear. It's a time to meet new people and learn some new things about yourself and life. Breathe deeply and exhale.

You'll first meet with the facility manager, or perhaps the same sales representative that you have been working with for the past few weeks or months. Of course there will be papers to sign, and you'll get the keys to her new unit. You can expect that the Manager will even walk you and Mom to her room/apartment to welcome her "home".

As you step into the entry way, adjust your concentration so it is back into work mode. Now it's time to ramp up your energies to unpack, and settle Mom in. You will be a tremendous help and strength in this chore, assuming that Mom still feels numb about the move. Both the facility manager and the movers will appreciate your business-minded way of ensuring the paperwork gets signed and the truck gets unloaded.

A few tasks you can expect to do on the "moving in" side are:

> Confirm proper mailing address for bills for Mom
> Obtain a new phone number for Mom
> Have WiFi connected and computer set up
> Ensure Cable TV is hooked up for the television
> Assemble emergency paperwork to keep behind the bedroom door

Set aside at least the rest of the day (or preferably a few days) to help Mom unpack her things. She'll appreciate the help, and may even look towards you to help her decide which cabinet to keep the glasses and which drawers to store her nightgowns. She's also likely to be scared, uncertain, lonely, even depressed in her new environment. Things may not go right or as smoothly as planned. Your smiling face will be a welcome distraction from the realization that her world has just turned upside down. Please, oh please, do not just drop her off and leave. Even I would cry if that happened.

As you leave Mom at the end of the day, don't forget to hug her tight. Remind her that things will be fine and that she will feel settled in in no time. She may sense that you are just trying to be positive. After all, how could you really KNOW that everything will be okay? Nonetheless, she will appreciate the efforts you are making to put her at ease. Remind her too, that you are just a phone call away.

Not everyone will get the opportunity to have Mom right by your side on this leg of her journey. For some, the simple reason that the move even has to occur is that Mom is no longer capable of understanding and/or participating in decisions and activities like these (think stroke, recent heart attack, etc.). Moving someone who has no cognition is a much lonelier process, when you are trying to help but have to make all the decisions by yourself. Appreciate any time you have with Mom involved, no matter how frustrating it may be at any particular moment. Then take time to reflect and share the love that is inside you.

There may be few loose ends to tie up once Mom is settled in to her new house. You may want to have a cleaning company do a thorough scrub of her old house, and donate any last items that did not make the trip. You may also still need to coordinate with the realtor on future showings and the sale of Mom's old house. Just as with any big project, there will always be a few strings that need cutting at the end.

Another reminder - If you are bringing Mom's own comforts from home (pictures, comforters/blankets, chair, etc.) into a residential setting where she does not have her own apartment, do make sure that each item is well labeled with your Mom's name, lest it be misplaced or lost.

My final advice on this part of the journey: Don't rush — in or out, physically or emotionally. This is a new chapter in Mom's life. The closing of one door; the opening of another.

It's been a big job, and a long day. Now it's time for you to go to your own house and rest.

Steps to Take

1. Make a list of everything that needs to be done when moving out of the old house –
   a. Forward mail
   b. Cancel utilities (phone, electric, gas, water, garbage)
   c. Cancel and return rented equipment (cable tv)
   d. Cancel newspaper
   e. Stop direct debits for bill payment if closing bank accounts
   f. Close bank accounts, if necessary
   g. Cancel yard service, only after house is sold
   h. Let house insurance company know that the house is for sale and that it will be vacant
   i. Make a note to cancel the house insurance upon sale of the house
   j. Leave the garage door openers with a trusted friend or with the realtor

2. Make arrangements for a trusted friend or the realtor to check on the house weekly if it will be left vacant.

3. Contact movers to hire, confirm dates, times, locations, etc.

4. Keep one suitcase of clothes, toiletries, etc. available for the next few days.

5. Make sure the boxes with bedroom sheets, blankets and pillows are well marked so that the bed can be made as soon after moving in as possible.

6. Make sure the boxes with bath towels, soap, etc. are well marked so that you can find them first.

7. Take a few extra rolls of toilet paper to the new house to make sure there is some on move in day (and the day after until you get to the store). You may want to leave a few rolls in the old house too (a nominal expense, but very appreciated if you are the one needing it!).

8. Take one last picture of Mom before you leave the house for the last time.

9. Look again, at each room of the house and in each drawer and cabinet to make sure you have not left anything.

10. On Mom's first night at her new house, make sure Mom is settled in with a bed, a bathroom, and her medications.

11. Exchange pertinent information with the facility staff so that they can contact you and you can contact them at a moment's notice.

Questions for Thought

1. Will Mom be at home when the movers come?

2. Who will be at the house when the movers come?

3. Who will be with Mom on moving day?

4. Consider having mail forwarded to your residence or to her power of attorney, especially if she is no longer able to perform financial management activities.

5. Does she need to open a new bank account (especially if she is changing cities)?

6. Consider adding yourself, or her power of attorney, to bank accounts for ease in bill payment.

7. Who will help Mom unpack and get settled in on her first few days?

8. Whose name will be given to the facility as the emergency contact person, especially to address issues on the first day and night?

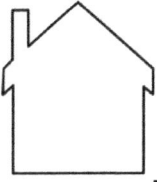

Chapter 7

New Beginnings

Your first day of school, your wedding day, the day your first child was born, January 1st, even today's sunrise. Each of these is a new beginning. Each of these holds a special memory. The same is true of Mom's first days in the "Home".

Remember your first day of high school, when you were terrified you'd get lost in the hallway on the way to your second class (the first class was easy to get to – you could arrive early and find your way)? Or when you were a kid and you had to make new friends? Now Mom is in that position. As adults we don't stop to consider how difficult such seemingly simple changes can actually be. But change is still change.

Your Mom is in new surroundings, with new people, embarking upon a new routine. It's going to bring about a little (or a lot) of anxiety. While she may be surrounded by dozens of other folks in her same age group, she can feel alone, out of place and certainly hesitant to just start up a new life. These people are not her friends (yet), the rooms are not the ones Mom is used to seeing, and even the food is not the same as what she was making at her old home.

The time it takes to adjust to a new environment gets longer and longer as we age. When you were a kid, you went from house to house and activity to activity rather quickly. Most times you jumped right in to the new environment, excitedly telling your parents at the end of the day all about the new kids you met and things you had done.

As you grew into your teenage years, you were a little more hesitant, and definitely self-conscious, especially when it came to changing schools and driving. You might have thought to yourself, "What if no one likes me? What if no one wants me in their group or on their team? What if I get lost driving in the city?"

We worry about different things, but we still worry. Somehow though, we manage to grow out of those years pretty much okay too.

Even as adults, starting a new job brought about anxiety. "What if the new boss demands too much of me? What if I don't understand the job? What if I am late because of all this stupid traffic!?"

For some, we might **still** be asking ourselves these questions! These feelings could last for months, or at least until we get our first performance review and figure out the best route to drive to the office.

You see, as you age, that process of change does not go away. And because there is so much more involved, it becomes more difficult. You are adjusting to the newness not just physically, but also emotionally, intellectually and spiritually too. You must do tasks in a new way, with a (sometimes fake) positive frame of mind, learning new skills and trusting in yourself (and God) that things will turn out for the best. You must believe that this change was done for the right reason and will result in the benefits you desire. But it will take time; time to adjust, time to learn, time to let go of the old, and time to feel comfortable with the new.

The same will be true for Mom.

After Mom's unpacking was done and the boxes no longer cluttered the living room, I expected that she would feel a bit more relieved. I thought she would be up early, puttering around her place, walking the halls saying "Hi" to all the new faces and meeting the staff. I thought she would be eager to check out the library, to fiddle with the machines in the fitness area, and of course to browse through the gift shop. I was excited for Mom's new adventure, Mom's new life.

Instead, when I arrived at her apartment the following Saturday, I found her just sitting in a chair, looking a bit uneasy and disoriented. It seemed as though she was afraid to get up and start moving, afraid to hang up the pictures, afraid to meet the neighbors across the hall. I was confused.

I asked her how she was feeling and at first she said she was "fine". Just fine. No further explanation, no elaboration, no more words. That's when I knew, she was NOT fine. I poured us each a cup of hot tea (my first step into relaxing), and went to sit beside Mom.

"What's going on?" I asked.

Mom replied, "I don't know. I don't even know where to start." She was whimpering. Not quite crying, but certainly not smiling either.

"What do you mean?" I pressed on.

Reluctantly, she whispered, "There's just too much that is new. I just don't know where to begin." ...

I waited. I knew there was more to come.

"In my old house, I didn't have to eat at a certain time. In my old house, I could drive myself to the store if I wanted something. In my old house, I could call my friend Felicya and she'd come over. In my old house, I didn't have to press some stupid button just to let everyone know I was up and out of bed."

That's when it hit me - the newness, the change. It was unwelcome because it brought about a lack of control, a loss of independence. With the move came the realization of a new, and somewhat stark, reality. Mom was aging. She needed to be looked after. She could not just simply do as she pleased anymore.

Mom was depressed. Perhaps not the clinical version, and certainly not with an official diagnosis, but the label we put on people when we see someone that is "down" or has "the blues". The move to a new Home had been brought about due to her deteriorating health. She was not viewing this as a new adventure, but rather as a place to just fade away.

I knew it would take Mom awhile to get herself out of this slump. But I also knew I could help. And I knew that my help was needed. On her own she was never going to pick herself up and start enjoying life again. She may never have learned about all the friendly people, the great activities, and the fabulous amenities her new home had to offer.

First thing up: developing a new routine. People like routine. As young kids, it kept us learning and out of trouble. As older adults, it gives us comfort and security.

We started with making a daily plan. The "Today" show is Mom's morning wake up call, that with a cup of coffee and perhaps an English muffin or a bowl of oatmeal. So why not keep it the same way. She enjoys it, it's healthy, and it keeps her in touch with the outside world (not to mention the latest dress, hairstyles and rock bands). I got the TV set up, her remote controls re-programmed for the right channels and her table and chairs where it would be comfortable for her to watch.

Next, we added in some physical activity to keep her muscles moving and the blood flowing (not to mention all the other physical and mental benefits a person will gain from exercise). The fitness room at her (resort style) Home was open 24 hours, but did not have a staff member on-site until 7 a.m. No problem. Mom was not going to miss the first part of the "Today" show to go work out anyway; her workouts would be around 9 a.m. Mom had worked out (meaning walk on the treadmill) sporadically over the years, but recently she had not made a consistent habit of it. With a bit of persuading, she admitted that she really did not have any good reason NOT to go. After all, she didn't even need to leave the building to get there. Her routine now includes ½ hour on the treadmill along with supervised weight lifting and flexibility exercises 3 days a week. Kudos for Mom; she's doing more than I do!

By the time she finishes up her morning "run", showers and dresses, it's almost 11 a.m. Perfect timing. Mass is at 11:30 a.m. each day. The Chapel is down the hall from Mom's apartment in a different wing of the building. She enjoys going to Mass every day, and by sitting in the same seat, she quickly made friends with the other ladies who sat near her.

The afternoon is when Mom would get the most "bored" or down. Sometimes she would eat her lunch up in her apartment, watching her favorite soap opera or "show" as she calls it. Then, at least for the first several months, I'm not sure what she did; time would just go by. However, once I got her looking at the activities schedule, and she began seeing some things pop up that she liked to do, it was only a matter of time until (with a little encouragement) she picked a few outings and gatherings each month to join in on. She found trips to parks, to the mall, and even to some city events and places. And on each trip, she also began to find some new friends.

Next on the routine were her dinner and evening plans. Dinner for Mom was going to be at 5:30 p.m. Although the formal dining area / restaurant opens at 4:30 p.m. (and there are people down there eating!), she has the luxury of waiting until later to eat. She found that if she watches the local news, then goes down to the dining room, that the rush is over and there is still plenty of time for her to leisurely eat without feeling like she is being hurried out the door. She can enjoy her meal and savor the flavors! The dining room closes at 7 p.m.

She tells me now that her first few nights downstairs to dine were the most uncomfortable. She didn't feel like she belonged, didn't really know anyone yet, and didn't feel like she could just insert herself into someone else's circle of ladies. The first few weeks that seemed okay. And then we both shifted our perception. Instead of always eating with the same folks, I encouraged her to sit with new people each day. Making new acquaintances, sharing stories and getting out of a strict routine were just what Mom needed. Soon she was looking forward to dinner – for the food and the conversations.

It took Mom a few weeks to get her routine down and smooth. She likes the predictability and repetitiveness of it and has really begun to blossom. Now when I stop by for lunch, she's anxious to introduce me to her new friends and chatter about the exciting times they just had taking the shuttle bus to the latest museum.

I'm happy, that she's happy.

Routines are the perfect way to get Mom settled and participating in her new life. She will feel the comfort of the consistency, and meet new people doing the same things she likes to do.

From a safety view, a routine is also great. The staff at the facility know where to expect to see Mom and when. If she's not there, they know something is up and they need to check on her. That's part of the reasoning behind pushing the "I'm OK" button each morning. It's all designed to let her keep her independence but still know that she is up and moving about. (By the way, if she does not push the button, someone will come check on her.)

Mom might see this requirement of "pushing a button" as an invasion of her privacy or simply a nuisance. You, on the other hand, should remind yourself, and her, that it is being done out of love, respect and safety.

Any one of us could slip and fall and need some help – not only those that have reached a magic age or have a certain medical condition.

To start a new routine, think of the A, B, C's: A for Actions, B for Benefits and C for Challenges. Taking Action is the beginning to any change. The action can be small or grand. It can be physical or simply a mental shift. Action can involve others, or be done alone. The point of action is to get moving, to **do** something, to get you out of your rut. Action is good for you, and it's good for Mom.

Find out what types of activities are available for Mom to participate in. No matter what her physical or cognitive impairment, there is likely to be at least a few activities that she can join in. Activities can range from something physical such as chair yoga to walking trips, or be something more creative such as art classes or poetry. Intellectual activities are available mostly centered on current events.

Don't let Mom tell you she can't participate, even if she is in a wheelchair or has some other physical restraint. She may still be able to use her arms, her legs, and her voice to join in.

Whether she can actively participate is only one part. She may enjoy simply listening to stories, watching TV or listening to songs on the radio. Even if she cannot communicate verbally, you will see her involvement in the way she taps her foot, nods her head or smiles. Use all of your senses to "see" what she is experiencing.

B is for the Benefits. There is a benefit to every action that we take. The benefit may be as small as just getting out of bed, or as large as developing a new hobby. For each activity or action that you identified above, list out the benefits. Use a multi-dimensional view. Benefits can be:

> Physical: moving about or getting fresh air
> Social: making new friends and interacting with others

Emotional: bringing joy to your day
Intellectual: learning something new
Spiritual: having a purpose and belief in yourself

The benefit in any activity is for the individual to decide. Each one of us may gain a different benefit from doing the same activity. There is at least one benefit to every action!

Challenges are things that keep us from taking an action. Challenges, like benefits and actions, can be small but seem very ENORMOUS. Challenges are the reasons we fall short, the excuses for why we stop participating. Challenges are our obstacles. Some may indeed be very big; others we just make that way so we can turn around and go back to comfortable corner.

Mom is very likely to throw you a whole laundry list of her challenges every time you suggest something new for her to try. Don't let her get away with this! Find ways to accommodate what she sees as her shortcomings. For every activity, there is some way to participate. Think again about the various dimensions: physical, social, emotional, intellectual and spiritual. Challenges are what make us grow; what make us thrive.

Challenges can, and sometimes will be, difficult. The struggle may seem too taxing, or take too much time. If that is the case, break it down into smaller parts. Even the challenge of getting out of bed can start by conquering the task of just sitting up. Overcoming a challenge is not easy, but it brings with it a sense of pride, success and worth. Start slow and work your way up.

Now let's put these A, B, C's together into Mom's new routine. Sit down with her one afternoon and have her start by picking out 3 activities that she would like to do during the upcoming month – one that she does each day, one that she will do each week, and one that she will do only once a month. Have her, mentally, set her disability to the side. If she could do anything, what would she want to do? Write it down on a list. Here are a few examples:

Daily activity: Going to the dining room for dinner

Weekly activity: Playing Bingo (or cards) with a group

Monthly activity: Going to a movie

Beside each activity, write the benefits. Be sure to include all or as many of the dimensions as possible. The benefit of simply getting out of one room and into another can bring joy and awareness.

Finally, write down the challenges, as Mom sees them, to each of the activities. Now think..... What accommodations need to be made for her to overcome these challenges? Rather than look at what is seemingly "impossible", find a way that it becomes "Possible!" Look at **all** the benefits to the activity. Just because a physical challenge presents itself, doesn't mean that Mom cannot benefit socially, emotionally, intellectually or spiritually. Every speaker enjoys a listener.

Now, let's put this together to form a routine – part daily, part weekly and part monthly. Work alongside Mom to encourage her, and help her see the benefits, even of the task of constructing a routine.

Encourage Mom to use the health club for fitness activities. Physical activities are a great benefit to her mind, as well as her body. It will also give her some exercise so that she is not sedentary. If even only for a few minutes (hopefully at least 10-15), a daily walk can get the blood pumping, get the energy up and lift her spirits. Many facilities also have trainers and exercise physiologists on staff to assist the residents with care and appropriate activities based on their level of fitness. For some, walking without holding on may be quite a challenge!

Get Mom involved in activities at the facility as soon as possible. But Caution! Do not rush this. Let her settle in at least for a few days after her move to get her mind (and her room) a little less cluttered. Then, review the list of monthly activities and pick one or two that she may want to start with. Encourage her to go to just these. She doesn't need to get involved in everything, and certainly does not need to have her schedule full every minute of the day! The sooner she gets involved in activities that she likes, the more adjusted and happy she will be at her new home.

As part of her routine, establish a calling schedule. You should call her each day for the first two weeks, then wean yourself (and her) off to a weekly, then bi-weekly timetable. These phone calls will be occasions that Mom will look forward to. The calls (or Skype) keep Mom excited about the days, gives her something to look forward to, and most of all – reminds her how much you care about her.

Depending on your proximity and your travel schedule, schedule visits every few months too. Stay for lunch or dinner. Walk with her outside on the grounds. Have her show you where things are – and what she has been up to lately. Many of the facilities will allow for family to eat with Mom. Just ask ahead of time and see if you can join her.

Help Mom select a suitable area in her entryway to keep her calendar and her schedule. This one designated spot for keys will also be part of her routine just like 'pressing the care button', taking her daily medications, and putting her name tag on her blouse each morning. If necessary, use post it notes or a typed out schedule or marker board for the days' or week's activities.

Encourage Mom to take advantage of the services provided by the facility. If there is shuttle service to the local retail or grocery stores, have her go – even if she doesn't necessarily need to buy anything. It is a great way for her to get out of her apartment, get some fresh air, and make some friends. This will also help her gain her independence back and let her feel as if she has options and control in her daily life. Even if she is in a memory care facility, there will be opportunities for her to go outside or to the store, accompanied by a caretaker.

Before you know it, Mom will have a plan and a routine. Her plan will give her structure for her day, her week and her month. And you can use it to start conversations each week too.

Remember, it all starts with Action. The more active she gets, the more involved she will be, and the better outcome (from all dimensions) she will have. Just follow the A, B, C's.

Along the way of starting her routine, Mom will make some friends (that's part of the reason, from the social dimension, that having a routine is advisable). However, making friends when you're in your 70's, 80's and 90's is not the same as when you were 5 years old.

Hopefully Mom will find a group of people that have interests, or backgrounds, similar to hers. The easiest way of doing this is by getting involved in the activities. If you are in the same activity, then presumably you both like that activity, and now you know you have at least one thing in common. Have Mom strike up a conversation with someone in the group, even if it starts as a simple "Hello" when she first sits down. A friendly, "that was nice, see you next time" comment is perfect at the end of the session.

With your Mom's new routine, she is likely to see the same people in the same places at the same times (yes, everyone else is building a routine too). This is a great way to connect and build some friendships. Encourage Mom to keep at it, and start small. She's not required to know everyone by name after only seeing them a couple of times.

If Mom is a bit more on the reserved side, you can help her make some friends by facilitating the introductions with others. Introduce yourself and Mom to facility staff and residents. Shake hands. It is likely your mom's actions will mirror yours.

Bear in mind, some of the residents may have lived at that particular facility for quite a while and may have already formed their own group and cliques. That's okay. In time, Mom will find her own circle of friends – some with the same interests, some that do the same activities or dine at the same time, or even some that have the same impairments or disabilities. Mom may warm up to someone quickly, or it may take her a while to get her bearings and feel comfortable. Others may be quick to take her into their crowd, especially if your Mom is open too. Remind her to be patient as she makes new friends. Good lasting relationships do not necessarily sprout overnight.

It is likely that once your mom has settled in for a day or so, the facility nurse will come by to do another functional assessment as well as ask a myriad of questions specific to Mom's health status. Medication lists will be reviewed. Current challenges and behaviors will be noted for future reference. Use this as a time for Mom to get to know at least one person (the nurse), and to ask about other people that might have some of the same interests as Mom. You should also ask about new doctors, if that is a need (such as if Mom is moving from out of town).

Essentially anyone that you meet, and anyone that Mom meets, at the Home, can become Mom's new friend. It may take Mom a few weeks or even months until she is comfortable getting to know others beyond the simple Hello's, but in time she will find where she fits in.

In the meantime, do not treat Mom like she in kindergarten. Good friends are hard to find, and she will eventually make some. No need to be condescending.

Don't forget, too, about Mom's 'former' friends from her old house. Encourage her to continue seeing them, inviting them to come by to show off her new Home, having them over for dinner or just a social visit. If it's possible, take Mom out to see her friends. Encourage her to chat with them on the phone (if dialing is problem, just ask the facility staff to help!). Although Mom has moved into a new house, she does not need to let go of her past- especially her friends. They were her friends before she moved, and there is no reason why they cannot continue to be friends forever. Maintaining these friendships will also help with her transition, and keep her spirits high.

A service that I see very under-utilized in senior communities is the complex shuttle service. With many seniors, moving into the community came along with giving up the ability to drive. To Mom, this means a loss of independence, a sense of failure, a disability of sorts. Convince Mom to think of it differently; instead, as a benefit. She no longer has to deal with traffic, no longer has to find parking, and no longer has to warm up her car on those cold winter days. You also know, on a more practical side, that you know longer have to worry about accidents and injuries (both Mom's and other drivers).

Encourage Mom to start off her new phase of life with a "driver". She may need to adhere to a schedule more than she likes, but with a little planning, she will still be able to get to the grocery store, to the mall, and out to meet friends. Her independence has not been taken away; her mode of transportation has changed.

Find out if the shuttle will only take Mom on scheduled trips for activities or to doctor's appointments, or if it is possible (for a fee or otherwise) for the shuttle to take her to church, to the movies or just to meet a friend for dinner. If not, consider other options including buses and taxis.

Part of a New Beginning also means setting things up for the future. When moving into a residential facility, you will need to fill out a great deal of paperwork. This will likely include a Power of Attorney for Finances and a Power of Attorney for Healthcare. From the facility view, a Will and other estate planning documents may not be needed, but packaged all together, this is an excellent way to get all Mom's affairs in order.

While she is beginning this new phase of her life, execute (or re-visit) her Powers of Attorney, her Will, and her beneficiary designations. Take the time (once she is settled) to have meaningful discussions with her about her end of life decisions. While I don't want to sound morbid, it really is the perfect time to discuss where to "draw the line in the sand" in terms of any final resuscitation and/or comfort care that she may want when the time comes. Remind her, that for everyone, a time will come – it's part of life. Take this opportunity to get your own affairs in order too. You never know when it will be your time, either.

Be cautious in this regard, though, but be persistent. She will still be in a vulnerable state, still actualizing her need to move into a senior community. While you don't want her to be overwhelmed with a "discussion of death" and the like, you also don't want her to wait so long that she no longer has the cognitive ability to share with you her thoughts and wishes. Be patient, but insistent. Listen to her thoughts, write down her directions, and have her sign it. You will both be happy you did.

Please don't think less of me for bringing up this subject, especially in this chapter. You know that every chapter has an end; and everything must end before a New Beginning can take place. By preparing now, and knowing that her legal affairs are in order, Mom (and you) will be able to start this leg of the journey, living the rest of her days Happily Ever After.

Steps to Take

1. Go on a tour of the facility with Mom.

2. Assist Mom in getting her keys, finding her way to the dining hall, activities room, etc.

3. Contact the concierge to see if there is a dinner companion and/or a welcoming committee lined up for Mom for her first dinner in the dining room.

4. If Mom is not outgoing, introduce her to the people she will likely have the most contact with – concierge/ doorman, dining room help, etc.

5. Get the activities list for the upcoming weeks and help Mom select 2-3 events she would like to participate in. Mark these items on her calendar.

6. Sit with Mom to develop a daily plan. Put it on paper.

7. Make follow up calls daily for the first few weeks, to see how Mom is settling in. Ask her what she has done that day, remind her of the benefits of the new home, and ask her what challenges she is having. Follow up with facility staff as necessary.

8. Review the safety and emergency procedures with Mom.

9. Introduce yourself to the staff, especially her nursing aides. Ensure they have your contact information in case of emergency.

10. Ensure that Power of Attorney documents have been executed. If Mom is no longer able to legally execute documents (she no longer has the cognitive capacity), then work with an attorney to establish a guardianship or other arrangement.

Questions for Thought

1. Who, from the family, will help Mom settle in?

2. Who, at the facility, will help Mom settle in?

3. Who will take Mom grocery shopping, etc. (if needed) during her first few weeks? How will these trips be arranged?

4. Who will drop by to visit Mom during the first few months?

5. Who will help Mom to get acquainted, make new friends, and participate in the social activities?

6. Who will go to the facility during the few months to see that the appropriate level of care is being provided?

7. What else can you do to help Mom settle in and get comfortable?

8. Can you incorporate her favorite colors into the rooms?

9. Do you want to have a house warming party for her? (this may depend on the type of facility)

Chapter 8

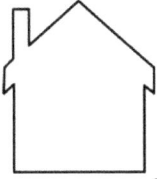

It's Not Over Yet

Helping Mom adjust to her new Home is the next part of your job. You've worked with her to get her new routine in order, to take advantage of the activities that are offered, and to make some friends. But she has only just begun. The ideas and plans are in place, now it's time to work that plan.

Alas, you've come to the next obstacle. You have some choices to make, the extent of which depends largely on how much time you have to spend with Mom and who else might be able to help you.

Before we just start forging ahead, remind yourself and Mom, that it takes patience, time, AND a step each day in the right direction.

Getting Mom all settled in is not a task that can be done in one day or even one week. Mom is dealing with a lot of change right now – change in her environment, change in her routine, change in her understanding that the realities of life are upon us. It will take her a few weeks or even a few months to feel relaxed and part of her new community.

Over a period of several weeks, I helped my Mom settle into her new place. I'd had some experience in this arena before, having moved my brother into a skilled nursing facility after he had suffered a traumatic brain injury.

But this was profoundly different. First, because it was my mom. Second, because she had not had an accident, but is merely "aging". Third, because Mom still does have her cognitive abilities, thus emotions were at play. And fourth, because she just has SO much stuff!

My brother had lost his cognitive abilities, so he was unable to participate in decisions. In a way, that was easier. I could just do what I believed needed to be done. I packed for him, unpacked for him and got his medical and emergency paperwork in order. While he did still have feelings, and periodic moments of clarity, for the most part he was like a child trapped in the body of a 42 year old man. However, that's a story for another day.

Mom is in the here and now. Her faculties are still very much in tact, and she definitely has an opinion on just about everything. She was not going to let me decide things on her behalf while she sat idly by. And I was happy about that. This was her new home; she needed to be involved in setting it up the way she wanted.

After unpacking the essentials, we took another tour of the facility and acquainted ourselves with the garbage room at the end of the hall (where all the empty boxes needed to go), where the Bistro Café was (so we could get something to drink while we finished unpacking), and where and when dinner was to be served. Then we rolled up our sleeves and began to organize the rest of her things. The majority of boxes had been sufficiently labeled prior to being put on the truck, so we were quick to sort the clothes from the dishes, the books from the towels. Slowly over a couple of days almost everything was put in its place and the empty boxes were disposed of.

Mom's closet took a bit of work; she has SOOO many clothes! For that job, I unloaded the clothes from the boxes, gave her a few suggestions on how to hang them, and then left her with the task of organizing them as she wanted. She is lucky in that she has three closets, including the one in the foyer. Due simply to her height (she's only 5' tall), I did help Mom put the lesser used things (those darn high heel shoes!) on the upper shelves. The rest of the sorting and arranging was her choice.

Dishes were another story. Mom is a collector. She has virtually every type of white Corellware dish ever made. And not just one, but either 4 or 6 of each set. Since I was not able to convince her to "let go" of many of these dishes, we needed to compromise a bit more when it came to keeping all of them in her new kitchen cabinets. With a bit of smooth talking and finesse, I persuaded her that she really only needed 2 of some of the dishes (and none of some others!) upstairs, with the rest being kept in boxes in the downstairs storage unit. The extras were still available if, and when, she needed them. (Note: to this day, she has never needed more than 2 of any one type of plate; she eats most of her dinners in the dining room.)

Fortunately, the rest of the kitchen set up was finished rather quickly. We had spent a lot of time sorting and discarding extra hand towels, pot holders and spices during the downsizing stage. Now it was just a matter of putting what she had brought on to the shelves and into the cabinets.

Moving on to the living room, the settling in took much longer. She decided to buy new furniture that fit more appropriately into the size of her new home. Mom was without all but a chair in the front room for almost eight weeks. It was all eventually delivered and a smile was on her face. The new apartment sized sofa, kitchenette table and chairs, and professionally designed curtains fit her style, and made her happy. Yet, she still (a year later) does not have the majority of her knick knacks out. Perhaps she never will, or maybe she is just taking her time. Either way, she knows they are in storage, and I'm waiting for her to decide when it's the right time to uncover them and put them in place. Her house, her time frame.

After Mom felt a bit more settled with her physical surroundings in her unit, I encouraged her to get involved in some of the activities we reviewed and put into action her new "routine schedule". Slowly, she began attending a few functions, had a reasonably good time (as she shared with me afterwards), and was gradually adding more to her calendar each month. Within another few months, she was sticking quite closely with her new routine, and seemed much more relaxed than I had seen her in a long time.

I'll be the first to share that not every day was full of joy. Mom had some bad times mixed in with the good. There were a couple of days when she called crying, telling me she was unhappy, didn't feel comfortable, and wished she had never moved. Those times were hard, for her and for me. I knew the change might be overwhelming, and had expected her to have some bitterness and even anger (at the situation). What I didn't expect was how sad and upset it made me feel to have her cry and to see and hear her so distraught. I knew, though, that I had a job to do. I needed to stay strong for her. I needed to remind her of all the good things that would come of this move. I needed to remind her that I loved her, and everything would be okay.

Mom pushed through the low points and has come out ahead in the end. She has developed and stuck to her daily routine of the Today show, exercise, Mass, outings and dinner in the dining room. She's pleased that we have our scheduled visits and quick Hello's on the phone. I go to most of her doctor's appointments with her, and take her out shopping every month. She smiles often now and is adjusting just fine.

Now it's your turn. Let's get to it. Let's help Mom get settled in and turn her house into a "home". Your task, as the son or daughter (or other loved one) is to help in making this a smooth transition for Mom.

It's likely that Mom hasn't moved in quite a while, so the thought of having to unpack by herself may not be appealing, let alone physically possible. Take care of the essentials first – set out her clean towels, load up the bathroom cabinet with toilet paper, and make sure her toothbrush and toothpaste are within easy reach at the bathroom sink. Then move on to the bigger things.

Help her hang her clothes in the closet and put her things in her drawers. Put glasses in the kitchen cabinets. Put pictures on the wall. Depending on how involved Mom is with these projects, let her direct where specifically she wants her belongings. Her choices may not be the same as yours – and it is her house!

As you are setting up the new place, don't be afraid to donate additional items (if Mom will let you) which no longer fit in the new environment. Although you may chastise yourself for even moving them in the first place, remind yourself, you didn't know how everything would fit until after you got Mom moved in. And if Mom still does not want to completely let go of some special items, storage is still a great option.

Help decorate. It won't feel like a real home to her until she has her "stuff" all set out, arranged the way she wants. It may just be the knick knacks that need positioning, or it might be new paintings that she needs to fill the walls. Whatever it is, she is bound to want at least some company, if not some help, in deciding which color, frame, or candle looks best. This task could take you a few minutes, or more likely a few months. No worries! The sooner its done, the more at home Mom will feel. But she has to like what is there. So let her take her time selecting just the right artwork for the entryway or pillow for the couch.

If Mom is in a facility that will do her laundry for her, then you will definitely want to label her clothes. Laundry tags or permanent marker for clothing (just like you had went you went to camp) work well to ensure that clothing gets back to the right person. Don't forget to label her other personal items too, including walkers, canes, blankets etc. You might also find it useful to take pictures of Mom with certain items such as her glasses, slippers, etc. That way you can better describe them if they do become lost.

A word of caution for those of you that have Mom in a skilled nursing facility, or any place where laundry is done for the resident. You will find out, sooner or later, that some items go into the dirty clothes hamper and for whatever reason are never seen again (perhaps lost with those unmatched socks?). If you are replacing clothes for Mom, or she is getting new ones as gifts, I suggest you not spend a lot of money on them. That is not to mean that the clothes should be "cheap" as in low quality. But do consider how much you want to spend on items that might only be worn a few times.

For a break in unpacking during the first day or so, take Mom on another tour of the facility. She will appreciate the change of pace for a few minutes, and it will be good to get her out of her own room and moving about. Let her become oriented with the layout of the floor she is on, and its proximity to the other common areas. Show her the nurse's desk, the dining hall, and the activities room. While you are out and about, inquire as to whether there are any new resident gatherings or programs. This would be a great way for Mom to get to meet other newer folks.

When you've got Mom settled into her new apartment, begin to encourage her to take part in the other activities that the facility offers. Encourage her to go on field trips, and participate in all kinds of social activities. If Mom has physical impairments, don't worry. In most homes, professional health aides will be available to accompany her. Depending on her health condition, you too, can take her on outings. Find a neighborhood coffee shop or park in which to spend a few hours. She will enjoy "getting out of the house" just as we all do – cabin fever can get to all of us!

As I mentioned earlier, the first few days of eating in the dining room can be an issue, albeit only a temporary one. Dining alone has a stigma associated with it. Even walking into a restaurant by yourself can be intimidating. Talk to the dining staff about seating Mom with another group. The companionship and the chatter will be appreciated. And if the simple thought of leaving the room to go eat by herself is stopping her, then ask the facility if there is an attendant or a companion that can come get her and eat with her at meal times. After a few times of going down by herself, she will become more accustomed to the process.

If Mom is not feeling well, or for some other reason does not want to make a trip to the dining room on a particular night, what alternatives exist? Can meals be delivered to her room? Can she pick up the meal earlier or later than regular dining times? Find out the possibilities and make sure that Mom understands them as well. Otherwise, she may fear that there is only one schedule that she must stick to or she goes without food for the night!

As part of the settling in process for both Mom and yourself, learn about the facility's protocol is in the event Mom has an emergency. Which hospital will she be taken to? When will you be notified, and how? Ensure the home has your current contact information for these types of events.

Another part of organizing Mom's new home is finding out who Mom is supposed to contact if she needs things fixed in her room or apartment. Is there someone to contact to hang pictures for her, and even to change the light bulbs? Find out too if the facility will let you install or bring other things from home. In an independent living arrangement, it may be possible to install a doorbell for Mom's apartment. Other facilities, especially assisted living and skilled nursing homes, will have restrictions on what can be done to the rooms. In addition, while the facility may allow pictures to be hung and/or shelves to be added, the physical work of doing so may need to be performed by the facility staff so as to ensure all safety and other codes have been adhered to.

As I mentioned in the last chapter, a nurse will be coming to visit Mom on a routine basis. Does Mom have the cognitive ability to orient the nurse? Or should you be there just in case? I suggest that for at least the first visit, you be present. Remember Mom's view of things may be slightly different than reality. In addition, she is likely to down-play any symptoms or difficulties she is having. The nurse is a new person, and Mom is going to put her best face on as a matter of pride. Meet the nurse in person, since you are involved in Mom's care and healthcare decisions. You are as much a part of Mom's care team as the professionals at the facility. You know Mom best, and will likely spend more time with her than the doctors. You can communicate Mom's preferences, likes, and challenges with her outside caregivers.

Physically now she is settled into her new Home. She is there; her things are there. However, mentally and emotionally, she may still take a while to "adjust" to the newness, and the change. Here are a few things you can do to help calm Mom's mind, as well as your own:

Check on Mom often. The first few days, stop by for a visit. Continue helping her set out her knick knacks, put up her decorations. Helping Mom organize her home can provide a sense of closure to you that the move has finally happened. It can also provide a sense of relief and less resistance from Mom. Help her unpack things bit by bit, talk about upcoming plans the facility has to orient her and for her to socialize.

If you can't physically be there, then call to check on her. And if she calls you, be sure to answer the phone. She needs to know that even if she is in a new place, you are still her rock, her stability. You need to let her know that you have not abandoned her.

Remind Mom that everyone in the facility has some type of debilitating issue (some similar to hers) so she will not stand out or seem out of place. Likewise, she will need to be patient with everyone else, just as they are patient with her.

Unannounced visits are great ways to tell if Mom is adjusting and if the facility is providing the care and assistance that they are required to. When you stop in, check the following:

Is the facility secured (or can anyone just come and go openly, including the residents)?

Does Mom appear to be well cared for? Clean, healthy (to the extent possible), active?

Is Mom's environment clean and orderly? Bed made, rooms clear from clutter.

When you go to visit, see if there is anything that you can help her with that will make you aware of her daily mindset. Have her tell you about her day's activities. Have her tell you about her plans for the upcoming week. Be sure to help her with the seasonal changes too. Keep her attitude and thinking in a "here and now" orientation.

Along the way, encourage Mom to express her feelings. You too can share your words of encouragement and concern. It will help both you and her to work on ways to relax or re-group when feelings of defeat become overwhelming. She may simply need you to "be" with her, to listen to her thoughts and to remind her that a deep breath and silent moment are all that is needed.

After a month or so, you will need to add a few more jobs to your check list. If Mom is on a monthly or quarterly food plan, be sure to check how she is managing it.   If she gets a set amount each month, what happens if she doesn't use it all? Work with her to ensure she uses up at least the amount that comes as part of the financial package. Otherwise, it is just lost money.

Find out how else she might be able to use this allocation. If it must all be spent on food at the facility, then she will need to buy more items from the bistro or restaurant. Are there things she can get that can be kept for days or weeks (bottled water, fruit, snack crackers)? Or can she invite guests for dinner and pay for their meals from her tab?

For fiscal responsibility, she should not "waste" any of the food allowance money by not using it. This makes sense on one hand, but is actually rather difficult in actuality. We were raised to save our money and be thrifty. As an example, fruit at the store is cheaper than in a restaurant. However, her food allotment is money already spent. She will lose it if she doesn't use it.

About now, and every quarter hereafter, is a good time for you to have a financial review with Mom. Let her know how much money she still has in her savings and investment accounts. Work with her to project an annual budget. There will be plenty of things for her in her new community, but some of them may cost money. Does she have extra to spend on field trips? Once she is settled into her new home, and the bulk of the one-time expenses are paid (movers, new furniture, etc.) let her know exactly how much she has and what a reasonable amount is available for her to spend each month and each year. It is her money, but it also needs to last at least as long as she does.

Monitor how she is adapting to her new environment. Is she getting down a new routine? Assess the new arrangement from a view of:

> Adequate level of Safety
> Appropriate services being provided
> Sufficient social interaction available and utilized
> Intellectual stimuli provided
> Emotional support from the staff

<u>I don't like it here!</u>

There will come a time, maybe after a few days, a few weeks, or even a few months, that Mom has a 'change of heart'. Although she agreed (or assented) to moving to her new home, now she's changed her mind. She tells you that she doesn't like it there, she feels left out, she's lonely, everyone ignores her, the people are mean, or a host of other adaption issues.   Do   not   worry.   This   is normal! It's akin to buyer's remorse. Only in this situation, you (and Mom) cannot simply return the product and get your money back.

You will need to work with Mom to get her over her anxiety and settled back into a routine in which she is comfortable and accepting of. She still may go through periods of not 'liking' it, but at least you will be prepared. And so will she. She may feel the let down after all the excitement of the move has passed. She may also be making herself feel bad by claiming that she should have settled in sooner. Work with her on these. They are just regular emotions.

In some instances, Mom may have outbursts where intervention is required. This could be happening as a result of her not "liking" the new facility. But more likely it is because of some other health reason. Nonetheless, you should find out what the process is for handling these matters. Is there a designated person that is used to mitigate the agitation? What is the protocol? Will they call you? What can you do to help?

Likewise, if there is something you know about that causes or escalates irritability in Mom, let the facility staff know when she moves in. In many institutions, the medical staff knows that outbursts and irrational behavior can be caused by Urinary Tract Infections (UTIs). But if you are aware of other issues specific to your Mom, then be sure to inform the staff. After my brother had his head injury, the ammonia level in his blood would occasionally become unbalanced. When this happened, he would act out and become combative. Knowing this, the facility was able to better treat and protect him, and the other residents, appropriately.

It may take up to a year for Mom to finally feel as if the new place is home. This is just like you and I when we moved into a new home.

As Mom is settling in, watch for signs of "Transition Trauma". It can be difficult for almost anyone who has to move. In the elderly, it may be even more important.   According to the Wisconsin Board of Aging and Long Term Care, Characteristics of Relocation Stress include:

Depression	Sadness	Crying
Despair	Confusion	Indecision
Apprehension	Anxiety	Restlessness
Sleep disturbances	Dependency	Insecurity
Distrust	Withdrawal/isolation	Loneliness
Negative comments about staff		Expressing concern
Being upset	Resistance	Unwillingness to move
Anger	Aggressiveness	Change in eating habits
Weight change	Stomach problems	
Hallucinations	Falls	

Take things slow and steady. Tell Mom often that she is doing just fine, and everything will work out the way it's supposed to in the end.

Watch for Abuse

We've all heard the horror stories of the abuse and neglect that can go on with the elderly and disabled in institutional settings. While I too wish it wasn't the case, do not put your head in the sand. Realize it is a possibility and take steps to ensure it is not happening in the setting that your mom is in.

Elder abuse and neglect (aka elder mistreatment) is defined by the National Center on Elder Abuse as, "intentional actions that cause harm or create a serious risk of harm (whether or not harm is intended) to a vulnerable elder by a caregiver or other person who stands in a trust relationship to the elder. This includes failure by a caregiver to satisfy the elder's basic needs or to protect the elder from harm."

No one wants to think about it happening, especially to our own loved ones. Don't limit yourself to thinking the abuse is only done by the staff; abuse can also be by other residents. Be aware of the types of abuse, and intercede if you suspect any problems. Do not fear being direct with the facility or the staff – after all, it is your Mom's life at risk. Types of abuse include:

Physical abuse or physical harm - physical interactions such as hitting, kicking, pushing, shoving, as well as inappropriate use of drugs or physical restraints.

Sexual abuse, including assault and unwanted touching

Verbal and emotional abuse, including emotional and psychological – verbal insults, threats, intimidation, humiliation, harassment. This also includes treating adults like children, isolation from family and others, and depersonalization of care.

Neglect by the caretakers – either deliberately or unintentionally. Ensure Mom is aware of the social schedule of activities that are available and who might come to get her to do certain types of things. For independent living, no one may be assigned, but for assisted living and skilled nursing someone should be coming to get Mom to include her in the activities of the day.

Indicators of improper care include over sedation, frequent urinary tract infections, diaper use when not required, body odor, uncombed hair, dirty or long fingernails, skin rashes, very dry skin, bruising, welts, dirty clothes, frequent emergency room trips, fear or reluctance to speak, unexplained weight loss, etc.

Isolated incidences may occur and may not always be avoidable. Your best bet is to inquire of the facility, what it does to prevent problems and how it handles the situation if, or when, it does occur. For any type of abuse, look into the specific situation at hand.

> What happened?
> Who was involved?
> What did the staff do to rectify the situation?
> Is there a problem resident? OR
> Is there a problem of control at the facility?
> Was a police report filed?
> How will the facility prevent a repeated incident of the same
> nature?

For any of these types of abuse, use your own personal observations to gather more information and report the matter to the facility administration. Unless you are visiting daily, you may not know if the particular action is a one-time situation or a repeated pattern. Report it at the first opportunity and expect that the facility will follow up properly to ensure that it does not happen again. If you believe the problem has not been rectified, or that additional outside intervention is needed, do not hesitate to contact your local Adult Protective Service agency.

Changes in care needs

Although Mom is only just now getting settled into her room, it's never too soon to inquire about the next steps. What if Mom needs a change in her level of care? This may be a reality soon, or not for a very long time. Either way, it's important to know and understand the process well before it is time to make those changes.

Keep in mind that if Mom needs additional services for only a specific reason (she had an injury that required care) then services may be able to be brought into her current location. Depending on the type of therapy or care needed, a short stay in a rehabilitation wing or specialized care unit may be warranted.

However, if Mom's health is declining to the extent that she needs continual additional service, then you may need to once again move her to a new place that is more appropriate for her care level.

If you suspect this will be needed in the near future, it would be appropriate to inquire at the onset of finding the right facility or location of Mom. Things to ask include in this regard are:

Can Mom have additional services brought in to her current apartment / room, including physical therapy, occupational therapy, speech therapy, assistance with Instrumental Activities of Daily Living?

What is the process for relocation in the same facility if an increased level of care is needed, such as 24-hour supervision, assistance with Activities of Daily Living?

Is there another wing or building for the increased level of care?

Who needs to initiate the re-evaluation process?

Who needs to initiate the move process?

How will you know when it is time to re-evaluated?

Who will move Mom and her belongings?

Whether this is an immediate concern, or one that you are simply anticipating, you should always be kept informed as to Mom's ongoing care level and needs. To accomplish this, the facility and Mom's doctors should provide you with information. Examples of this include written reports from the facility and doctors, periodic follow up assessments and reviews. If you believe another assessment is needed and the facility has not already expressed concern, then you have the right to request a re-evaluation as well.

Bottom line: do not just be an idle bystander. Take part in Mom's care.

Health care directives, End of Life Decisions

Just a reminder, if you still have not done so, have the discussions with Mom about her end of life care. Have her put in writing if she has any health care directives, her end of life decisions and her Will. Be gentle with each of these. While they are important, you will want to make sure that you don't cause Mom additional stress by focusing on the fact that one day she will be dead. Make it be all part and parcel of her settling into her new home, as opposed to this new home being one step closer to her being in the grave. (That is definitely too gruff!)

Don't feel guilty or morbid about the need for these preparations though. Mom would not be at this stage of her life, and would not need to live in a supportive living environment if she was fine and healthy. We all know that at some time our lives will come to an end. The transition to the Home is a perfect time to address these final end of life decisions, if you have not done so already.

Ask Mom what her thoughts are as to when her care should end. If the circumstances arise, does she want to be resuscitated? Does she want to be on any life support systems? Would she want any additional surgeries (assuming she is an appropriate candidate for such) to continue or improve her care after such an event? Or does she simply want "comfort care" and pain medication to last her until her final days?

Memorialize her wishes in an Advanced Directive or a Physician's Order for Life Sustaining Treatment (POLST). Be sure these directions and preferences are contained in the Emergency papers that are on the back of the door in Mom's bedroom and/or maintained by the facility staff. Have a copy for yourself, as her closest family member, too.

Take a few minutes to talk with Mom too about her wishes for after she has died. Does she want to be buried or cremated? Does she have a specific funeral home picked out? Knowing Mom's wishes now will alleviate the stress that comes with the moment that Mom does pass away. You will know what Mom would have wanted and be able to fulfill her last wishes as best you can. The facility may be able to assist you in having her body taken to a local funeral home for preparation.

Finally, have Mom draft and sign a Will. Make sure that you and/or the Executor of the Will has a copy. The facility does not need a copy of this.

Take a few minutes now as well to find out from the facility as to what will happen to her apartment / unit when she dies? Who will need to clean out her belongings and how long will you have to dispose of her things. Knowing all of these things now, will lessen the physical and emotional challenges you will be going through when the time does come.

Winding up someone's life after they have died is a whole separate discussion, but it's wise to have elements of that talk with Mom while she is still alive and able to participate.

The most important thing to helping Mom settle in, is just to be there with her. She may not talk; she may not even want to interact. But she will want you there, even if she doesn't tell you directly. My request: Be there for her; just be there.

Steps to Take

1. Set up a weekly call schedule

2. Visit Mom monthly for the first several months, then taper off to quarterly, etc.

3. Drop in on Mom unannounced a few times – to check on her status, and how the facility is treating her.

4. Schedule doctor appointments, dentist, etc. or confirm that these are handled by the facility.

5. Ensure she is getting out – grocery store, clothes shopping, access to items she needs. If there is not a van service to do this, then make scheduled arrangements (weekly, monthly?) to do these things.

6. Check back with Mom to see that she has put out her knick knacks, hung her pictures, etc. She may have wanted to "get settled in" (mentally and emotionally) first, so don't let her go too long without making the place her "home".

7. Help her decorate for the holidays during the first year. Get new decorations if needed and help take things up and down to the storage room.

8. Check in on how Mom is using and tracking her meal allowance. Help her find additional ways to spend the account if needed.

9. See if Mom is getting involved in activities. Learn what her favorites are, and what she doesn't like too.

10. Ask if Mom is using the fitness services.

11. Evaluate if additional services need to be added (that don't already come standard).

12. Make sure her health, and room and board billings are correct and being paid.

13. Check on Mom from a social/emotional view – is she getting what she needs in those areas? The attention she needs?

14. Ensure Mom has your phone number programmed in to her phone or that it can be easily found.

15. Confirm contact information and procedures if there is a medical emergency.

16. Designate one person for the facility to call (and a back-up person) in case of medical emergencies.

17. Go with Mom to medical appointments to fully understand her health situation.

18. Prepare end of life documents and make funeral preparation. Have discussions with Mom; write out her wishes in a POLST and a Will. Consider pre-paying for funeral expenses.

Questions for Thought

1. Who will be the main point of contact if Mom has a medical emergency?

2. Who, in the family, will be the primary overseer? The one that looks in on Mom to see that she is being taken care of? That she is receiving the level of care she needs?

3. Who should Mom call if she needs anything, including just to talk?

4. What are you going to do if Mom gets upset and wants to leave or go back to her hold home? What instructions can you give the facility to help calm Mom down?

5. Who will be the main person to report (or discuss) any abuse that you might observe?

6. Who will go to Mom is there is a medical emergency? Is there a back-up person for when the primary contact is on vacation or out of town?

7. When will you need / want to re-assess Mom's care? Who will do this?

8. Who will go with Mom to medical appointments?

9. Who will be the point of contact for end of life decisions?

10. What type of continued information do you want from the facility? Who will it be sent to?

11. Who should you call if you have questions on her care? Or important information that the facility needs to know about?

Chapter 9

Now I Can Sleep

Ahhh… Now, I can sleep.

It's been six months since Mom moved into her new home. Almost a year has passed since we began this journey. The long and winding road is finally coming to an end, and Mom is finally settled in to her new place.

While physically she's living in her new place, and her belongings are with her, it still may take a few more months before she truly feels like it is her "home".

For all of us, a move into a new house can be traumatic. It certainly is a significant change in our lives. It's not uncommon to feel overwhelmed, out of sorts, even angry. These effects are multiplied in an older person, especially if she was not looking forward to the move anyway.

I could tell when Mom finally felt as if she was settled in to her home when she started declining my offers to come over, in favor of her spending time doing activities with her friends. When we did agree on a day for me to visit, Mom greeted me eagerly, ready to show me the changes she had made in her apartment – the decorations she had put up, the candles she had set out, even the hand knitted afghan she had laid out on the couch. She was pleased with herself for making these seemingly small additions and adjustments. She was happy.

As I walked in, she motioned (politely directed) me to a particular chair, then she found her own comfortable spot on the sofa. She had her television remote on the table in front of her place, and a tea cup on a coaster. She was cheerful, dressed in a brightly colored top and slacks. She was ready to share with me the adventures of the past few days.

This was a far cry from the last time I was over. Only a couple weeks before, I dropped by to see how things were. Mom was sitting slumped at her table, no make-up on, hair not combed, clothes on but in disarray, wearing the old gray sweat pants style of lounge wear. You know the kind that screams, "Leave me alone, I want to be grumpy!" She seemed like she didn't care about anything. Her apartment had papers piled on tables, blankets just thrown on the couch, and dirty glasses on the counter. It looked like she hadn't bothered picking up for several days. And she looked sad.

A stab of guilt ran through my heart, and I sighed. But before I could question myself, I regained control. I reminded myself, "Mom's here because it is the best place for her. She is well cared for and safe. I helped her move here because I love her."

I worried about Mom for the first several months, until finally during these last couple of weeks I saw a shift occur. I had been told that it could take up to a year for her to feel settled in. Really settled in, that is. And now she was. I wanted to hug her and tell her how happy it made me feel that SHE was happy.

I still worry sometimes when the phone rings at an odd time in the evening and I see Mom's name pop up on the caller id. My heart skips a beat or two as I answer, and anxiously ask, "Is everything okay?"

"Of course" says Mom. She just wanted to remind me to pick up some berries on my way in to see her tomorrow.

"I will, Mom." I say, glad that she is back to being the Mom I know and love.

So what can you do to ensure Mom is settled in and to keep her with her energy high and her spirits even higher? Here's a few ideas:

Be patient, be understanding, be strong. This is not to say jump at Mom's every beck and call. And believe me, she'll have them. But when she does call, remember that it takes her a longer time to adjust than you might realize.

Set up your routine – calls to Mom on Sundays, visits the first weekend of each month. Find the balance between your life, your own family and Mom. Do not forget, they are all important parts of your world.

Keep your call schedule. Taper off a bit so your calls are a little less often, perhaps only every few days for a few minutes at a time. Be sure though, that the calls still take place. These may be just what Mom needs to keep her going from week to week. During your scheduled phone calls, have her fill you in on what's new with her, what activities she's done lately and what she plans on doing in the upcoming weeks. Inquire as to when her next doctor's appointments are, how she has been feeling and if she is comfortable. Ask her if there is anything you can get for her or do for her. Let her know that you are still a big part of her life, and that you are happy that she is adjusting well.

Keep up with the visits too. Stay with Mom for lunch or dinner a few times a year. She'll be pleased to show you off - you're her child! Even if you don't want to eat along with her (I can agree that pureed food is not that appetizing), but just having you there as company will be comforting for her.

Sure, Mom may still call you a few times outside of planned visits. Ask her how she is and really listen to her answers. Listen to her tone of voice, listen for the sadness. She may have called simply to hear your voice, to "connect" with you if she is feeling lonely. Find out, if you can, why she is restless or anxious. Try to alleviate her fears with kind words of encouragement. Remind her that everything is okay, and you are only a phone call away.

Holidays will be extremely emotional times, especially during the first year. Ensure that Mom is not alone on these days. If you cannot be at her place, and she cannot come to yours, try to find a friend that can go to visit with her. Find out about activities at the facility, and make plans to have her participate. Talk it up, get that excitement back just like when you were young. Each holiday is a celebration – a celebration of love and of life.

After a while, Mom will have developed her own routine. Do not interfere with it. Repeat: Do NOT interfere! Mom will have her own plans and her own activities, and you should adjust **your** schedule to accommodate. I realize that you might not think that her schedule is much – it may only include one activity a day, or even one every few days – but it is still Mom's routine, and if she's happy with it, then that is what matters.

And just like you and me, she will have her up days and her down days (probably when it's gray and rainy). These are normal, just as she had before she moved. She's less likely to take it out on you if she's adjusted, and if she knows of some alternatives to keep her busy on those long, cold days during the winter months.

So how often do you really need to check in on Mom? That is entirely up to you. I'd suggest no more often than once a day, preferably once a week at most. Let her have her freedom now that she's settled in. Be comforted by the fact that the facility has your contact information in case anything goes wrong. Likewise, Mom needs her individuality back to live her life – without you breathing down her neck. Be available if she calls, but let her rope out a little so that she can learn to make her own decisions again. You may not agree with some of the things that she picks to do, but then again, you probably didn't before either.

If Mom doesn't call you for a few days or even a few weeks, that's great! That means she's adjusted. She's found her routine, her friends, her activities. Don't be worried about her. Either she will or the home will call if there are any emergencies or issues. In fact, in this instance, no news IS good news!

Also don't forget to keep Mom up to date with what's happening outside her new environment too. Let her know how you are doing, how the family is, what the kids are up to. Keep her in touch with family and friends from her old neighborhood. Be sure those people have her new address so they too can send her cards and letters.

You may still worry about Mom, especially her safety. That's natural. After all, you worried about her before she moved in to the Home. Now, you'll worry less. There will still likely be accidents – hopefully only minor ones. But Mom IS in the best place she can be for her own health, protection and safety.

Now take some time to enjoy this new phase of your life too. Caring for an aging parent can be a challenging task, physically and emotionally. Remind yourself that you did the right thing. You love your Mom, and it shows.

Life is precious. Take care of those you love.

Steps to Take

1. Set up a weekly/monthly call schedule for calling Mom.

2. Set up monthly or quarterly visits to ensure you (and her) are satisfied with her care and her comfort.

3. Review Mom's status with facility staff at least quarterly, if Mom is not relaying much information and/or you cannot get out to visit.

4. Continue to drop by unannounced to check in on Mom and the facility.

5. Continue to go to medical appointments with Mom.

6. Find out what continuing correspondence the facility will require from you, and what they can provide to you.

1. Is there any other information I need to let the facility know?

2. Is there any other information I need to know about the facility or Mom's care?

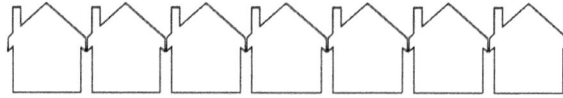

Life is precious. Take care of those you love.

Additional Resources

AARP.org

Administration on Aging – www.AoA.gov

A Place for Mom.com

Assisted Living Facilities.org

Assisted Living Federation of America

Benefitscheckup.org

Eldercare.gov

Helpguide.org

SeniorHomes.com

Senior Housing Net.com

Senior Living.com

Senior Outlook.com

National Center for Assisted Living

U.S. Department of Housing and Urban Development – www.hud.gov

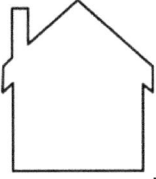

Glossary

Accreditation: A process of formal recognition that certifies a senior housing or service provider. An accreditation means that a provider has been thoroughly evaluated and meets set requirements and quality standards.

Activities of Daily Living (ADLs): Basic tasks of everyday life that include dressing, bathing, eating, transferring (for example, from bed to chair) and toileting.

Administration On Aging (AOA): An Agency of the U.S. Department of Health and Human Services that serves as a federal level advocate for older persons and their concerns. AoA encourages and coordinates a responsive system of family and community based services throughout the nation.

Administrator: A person responsible for the day-to-day management and operation of a health care or assisted living facility.

Adult Day Care: Daily structured programs in a community setting with activities and health-related and rehabilitation services to elderly who are physically or emotionally disabled and need a protective environment. This care is provided during the day, with the individual returning home for the evening.

Adult Protective Services: A public agency that investigates reports of abuse and neglect of vulnerable adults. APS usually works with local law enforcement. Immediate dangerous situations should be directed to 911 or local police.

Age-Associated Memory Impairment: A normal mild memory loss that increases with age; not to be confused with forms of dementia.

Aging In Place: A concept that allows a senior to live in his or her home for as long as possible.

Ambulatory: The ability to be mobile (walk), not confined to a bed or hospital.

Area Agency On Aging (AAA): A national network of state and local programs that provide seniors with information and referral services for in-home services, counseling, legal advice, adult day care, skilled nursing care/therapy, transportation, personal care, respite care, nutrition and meals.

Assessment: The process of documenting a person's mental, emotional, and social capabilities, usually in measurable terms and performed by a physician.

Assisted Living: A housing option for seniors who cannot live independently and need help with medications and daily living activities, such as bathing, grooming, eating, dressing and going to the bathroom. In general, a state-licensed program offered at a residential community with services that include meals, laundry, housekeeping, medication reminders, and assistance with Activities of Daily Living (ADLs) and Instrumental Activities of Daily Living (IADLs). The exact definition will vary from state to state. Generally regarded as one to two steps below skilled nursing in level of care. Typically, residents in an assisted-living arrangement have individual service plans tailored to their care needs. Staff members are on site 24 hours. In some states, residences are licensed and required by law to provide specific types of help.

Assistive Equipment: A selection of equipment and products intended to allow elders and/or people with disabilities to live more independently. Examples include walking aids, communication devices, elevated toilet seats, and special telephones for people with hearing impairments.

Assisted Transportation: Rides provided to aging or disabled people who need help getting to appointments and other necessary places. Programs include door-to-door van service, volunteer drivers and escorts, and discount taxi programs.

Audiologist/Audiology: Healthcare professionals specializing in identifying, diagnosing, and treating hearing impairment or hearing loss.

Caregiver: The primary person in charge of caring for an individual with special needs. This person is usually a family member or designated healthcare professional.

Care Manager: A person who assesses, organizes and monitors long-term care services for patients; usually a nurse or social worker.

Care Plan: A document that outlines the basic care and services a patient needs for his or her individual health problem; prepared or approved by a doctor.

Case Management: A planned approach to the coordination of health services to individuals.

Companion Care: Also referred to as Supervision Respite, this service provides home based care of seniors while the family caregiver is on a short term absence.

Continuing Care Retirement Community (CCRC): Housing planned and operated to provide a continuum of accommodations and services for seniors including independent living, assisted living, and skilled nursing care, usually on the same campus. A CCRC resident contract often involves either an entry fee or buy-in fee in addition to the monthly service charges, which may change according to the medical services required. Entry fees may be partially or fully refundable. The fee is used primarily as a method of privately financing the development of the project and for payment for future healthcare. CCRCs are typically licensed by the state. This community is commonly called Life Care.

Custodial Care (Personal Care): The supervision and/or assistance of activities of daily life offered in the home environment. This is a 24-hour program for an individual who does not desire to live in a congregate home. Care for individuals who need assistance with non-medical activities of daily living. Professional training is not required to administer this type of care. Custodial care is not covered by Medicare; Medicaid coverage is extremely small.

Dementia: A progressive loss of mental ability affecting memory, judgment and cognitive powers severe enough to interfere with the normal activities of daily living.

Discharge Planner: A person, usually a social worker, who aids hospital patients in transitioning from a hospital setting to another form of health care such as home care or a long-term nursing facility.

Elder Abuse: A term used to describe one or more of the following: physical, sexual, financial or emotional abuse of an elderly person (65 or older). The term can also refer to the isolation, neglect and self-neglect of an elderly person.

Elder Care: Elder care encompasses a wide range of services that can be administered in various settings including homes, assisted living facilities and skilled nursing facilities. Elder care is usually provided over a long period of time and includes health-related services, supervision, and a wide range of personal and social services.

Emergency Response Systems: An automatic response system for medical, or other emergencies triggered by electronic monitors on a person or in a home.

Estate: A term meaning all of a person's property, entitlements and obligations at the time of his or her death.

Geriatric Care Manager: A health care professional trained to work with seniors. Care Managers assist individuals and their families in creating and implementing a care plan to meet the individual's medical and financial needs. A professional who performs an assessment of a person's mental, physical, environmental and financial conditions to create a care plan to assist in arranging housing, medical, social and other services.

Geriatrics: A subspecialty of medicine that focuses on health care of the elderly, to prevent and treat diseases associated with getting old.

Home Care Services: Assistance given to persons in their own home. This assistance can either be in the form of household activities such as cooking, cleaning or doing laundry or it can be in the form of health care activities required for daily living or necessary medical procedures.

Home Health Aides: Persons who provide every day care to individuals in their own living environment. State requirements vary, but services are considered to be non-medical and usually relate to performing daily living activities, doing minor household chores and medication management.

Hospice Care: Professionally coordinated support services, including pain and symptom management, social services, and emotional and spiritual support for terminally ill people and their families. The care is provided at home and in other settings.

Home Health Care (Home Care): Health-related services such as nursing; social work; occupational, speech or physical therapy; and personal care provided in the home. Usually for patients recovering from an acute illness or chronic debilitating conditions.

Homemaker Services: Household activities such as cooking, cleaning, laundry and shopping that are performed by another person because the homeowner is unable to perform them. In most states, homemakers are not certified to perform hands-on care.

Independent Living: Communities offering an independent lifestyle and specific services and amenities that cater to senior citizens and promote active, healthy senior lifestyles for the golden years. Independent living is not an option for someone who cannot care for him/herself.

In-Home Assessment: The evaluation of an individual at their house instead of in a different setting.

Incontinence: The loss of voluntary control over excretory functions (urination, bowel movements or both).

Institutionalization: To commit or place a person into an institution. Usually happens in situations in which persons are no longer able to care for themselves because of mental illness or health problems.

Instrumental Activities of Daily Living (IADL): A level of activities that are secondary to basic functions, but are important for independent living. These include: paying bills, grocery shopping, driving and managing finances, telephone use, housekeeping, preparing meals and taking medications correctly.

Long-Term Care: Health care and support services provided to those who are not able to fully function independently for long periods of time. Provision of services to persons of any age who are afflicted with chronic health impairments.

Long-term Care Insurance: A privately issued insurance policy which covers the cost of nursing home care, assisted living, and home health care. Premiums are based on age, health, length of deductible period, amount paid, and duration of benefits.

Medications Management / Medication Administration: Formalized procedure with a written set of rules for the management of self-administered medicine, as in an assisted living setting. A program may include management of the timing and dosage for residents, and could include coordination with a resident's personal physician. The resident must take the medication him or herself. For instance, the community can remind the resident that she needs to give herself the medicine injection, but the community cannot perform the actual injection itself.

Medicaid: The Federal and State jointly funded medical and financial long-term care program for people with limited income and assets, the disabled, and the elderly. It is administered by the states within federal guidelines. Eligibility and coverage may differ from state to state. For long-term care services, states have additional eligibility rules.

Medicare: Nationwide medical insurance program administered by the Social Security Administration for individuals age 65 and over and certain disabled people, regardless of income. Provides for hospital and nursing facility care (Part A), and physician services, therapies, and home health care (Part B).

Memory Care: Self-contained environment specifically designed to serve residents with Alzheimer's disease or related dementias.

Nurse Assistant: Individual who provides most of the personal care and assistance with daily living activities to residents. A Nurse Assistant must be certified to provide care in nursing facilities that participate in the Medicare and Medicaid programs. A Nurse Assistant (or Certified Nursing Assistant, CNA) works under the supervision of a Registered Nurse or Licensed Practical Nurse.

Nursing Home: Also referred to as a Skilled Nursing Facility. A state licensed facility that provides 24-hour medical and nursing care and rehabilitation activities for residents, room and board, and activities for convalescent residents and those with chronic and/or long-term care illnesses. Regular medical supervision and rehabilitation therapy are mandated to be available, and nursing homes are eligible to participate in the Medicaid program. All or part of a nursing home may participate in Medicare and/or Medicaid and if "certified" they are also subject to federal laws and regulations.

Occupational Therapy: Process to help individuals relearn activities of daily living and increase self-reliance. It is generally administered by a licensed therapist, who teaches people to compensate for functional limitations.

Out-of-Home Care: Any place, institution or facility where a person is living and receiving care, that is not the residence they grew up in or lived in prior to moving to their present location. Typical examples include Nursing homes and Assisted Living Facilities.

Palliative Care: Professionally coordinated services that focus on physical, mental, social and spiritual needs of those with life-threatening illness and their families. The goal is to maintain the highest level of comfort.

Paratransit Services: Also known as Dial-a-Ride, provide special transportation services that are available for seniors and other people with disabilities. Most paratransit vehicles are equipped with wheelchair lifts or ramps to facilitate access. Services act as an alternative mode of flexible passenger transportation to senior centers, medical care, shopping malls, or specific appointments.

Patient Assessment: A standardized instrument which allows a nursing home to establish a patient's abilities. It is used in determining the level and type of assistance the patient needs, as well as establishing a plan to help the patient improve or regain abilities. This is also referred to as a resident assessment.

Personal Emergency Response System: A portable electronic device that enables a user, through the press of a button, to receive 24-hour help services in case of a fall or other medical emergency.

Physical Therapy: The treatment of a disease or injury, by physical and mechanical means (as massage, regulated exercise, water, light, heat, and electricity.) Physical therapists plan and administer prescribed physical therapy treatment programs to help restore the patient's function and strength. The process includes individualized programs of exercise to improve physical mobility, and is often administered following a stroke, fall, or accident. Physical therapy is generally managed by licensed physical therapists.

Primary Caregiver: An individual who accepts and takes on the primary every day duty of caring for the needs of another individual. This role is typically taken on by the spouse or adult child of the individual who requires care.

Primary Care Physician: The doctor an individual will see first for most health problems. This doctor is trained in basic care and will make sure the individual will get the care he or she needs to stay healthy. This doctor may talk to or refer you to other specialists as needed. Many health plans require that you consult your primary care physician before seeing any other doctors or healthcare providers.

Private Pay Patients: Patients whose care is paid for from a private source instead of by a governmental program such as Medicaid, Medicare, and Veterans Administration. The private source can be the patient herself, her family or another third party such as a private insurance company.

Quality Care: Care and services that allow an individual to attain his or her highest functioning level as possible. Functioning level refers to the highest level of mental, physical, and psychological function that can be achieved in a dignified and caring way.

Rehabilitation: Therapeutic care for an individual requiring intensive physical, occupational, or speech therapy.

Resident Care Plan: A specific written document that defines the plan of care for nursing facility residents that will meet all of the resident's specific needs. The plan is developed by an interdisciplinary team and contains specific measurable objectives and time requirements for provided services.

Residential Care Facility: A long term care environment that provides supervision or assistance with activities of daily living. The environment may be a group home, specialized apartment complex, assisted living facility, skilled nursing facility or any of a number of other types of institutions that provide care services where individuals live.

Retirement Community: An age-qualified housing community. Amenities and services are often shared within groups of residents. There are various types of retirement communities based on the preferences, abilities and supportive needs of the senior.

Respiratory Therapy: The treatment of diseases that relate to the lungs or cardiovascular system. The primary goal is to assist patients with breathing difficulties, reduce fatigue and increase a patient's tolerance in performing daily activities.

Respite Care: Support services which provide temporary relief to those in charge of care services to individuals. Respite care is also known as caregiver relief, as it can provide the impaired person's caregiver with needed time away from the patient. This type of care can last from several hours to several days and can be provided in-home or in a residential care setting.

Self-Neglect: A condition in which an individual fails to attend to their own basic needs, such as personal hygiene, appropriate clothing, feeding, tending appropriately to any medical conditions, and reasonable financial management.

Senior Apartment: Age-restricted multi-unit housing with self-contained living units for older adults who are able to care for themselves. Usually no additional services such as meals or transportation are provided.

Senior Centers: A place in a community where seniors can gather for support, socialization, fitness and/or other services provided for older people, meals, recreation, classes public benefits counseling, information and referral services, employment services, volunteer opportunities and more.

Skilled Nursing Care: Any care service that must be done by, or under the supervision of, a Registered Nurse. Intravenous injections, tube feeding, and changing sterile dressings on a wound are examples of skilled nursing care.

Special Care Units (SCUs): Facilities within nursing homes and residential care facilities that have special accommodations for persons with Alzheimer's disease or related dementia. Special Care Units (SCUs) exist to better meet dementia residents' needs and to protect residents without dementia or Alzheimer's.

Speech Therapy: A service designed to help people overcome speech and communication problems such as speech difficulty following a stroke, aphasia, swallowing difficulties and voice disorders. Some of the costs of speech therapy may be covered by Medicare as long as the patient meets the requirements.

Telephone Reassurance: Calls that are typically made at a predetermined time of day by agencies or volunteers to an elderly person. The purpose of these calls is to check up on the elderly person, while at the same time offering reassurance, contact and socialization.

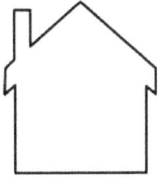

Amy K. Atcha is a Legal Guardian and Power of Attorney for aging and disabled adults, Speaker and Author.

She is an experienced presenter and seminar leader, having delivered hundreds of keynote speeches and breakout sessions. Amy's workshops and consultations emphasize "person-centered" care. Her dynamic and sincere presentations benefit the individual, family caregivers, the employer and service providers.

Amy is a National Certified Guardian. She has also earned designations as a Certified Employee Benefit Specialist, Certified Fraud Examiner and Certified Public Accountant. Amy is a notable member within the National Guardianship Association, the National Speakers Association, and Toastmasters International.

Amy's goal is to leave her clients, and their families, feeling prepared and ready for what life may bring.

Amy's other books include:

ME: Facts & Forecasts, A Guide for Now and Later, Written by YOU with help from Amy K. Atcha

When Crescent And Cross Converge, Lessons in Life, Love & Respect

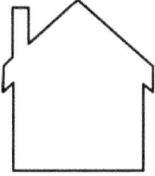

For More Information

Customized Caring, Inc.

901 Indigo Court
Hanover Park, Illinois 60133
www.CustomizedCaring.com

Contact Amy K. Atcha
at
630.306.4480
amy@customizedcaring.com

Life is precious. Take care of those you love.

www.ingramcontent.com/pod-product-compliance
Lightning Source LLC
LaVergne TN
LVHW061223060426
835509LV00012B/1398